JADED

FROM THE EDGE

BOOK THREE

BY EVIE RILEY

Sale of this book without a front cover may be unauthorized. If this book is coverless, it may have been reported to the publisher as "unsold or destroyed" and neither the author nor the publisher may have received payment for it.

No part of this book may be adapted, stored, copied, reproduced or transmitted in any form or by any means, electronic or mechanical, including photocopying, recording, or by any information storage and retrieval system, without permission in writing from the publisher.

Thank you for respecting the hard work of this author.

JADED

FROM THE EDGE

BOOK THREE

COPYRIGHT © 2022

EVIE RILEY

SECOND EDITION

ISBN: 978-1-77357-694-7

PUBLISHED BY NAUGHTY NIGHTS PRESS LLC

COVER ART BY WILLSIN ROWE

NAMES, CHARACTERS AND INCIDENTS DEPICTED IN THIS BOOK ARE PRODUCTS OF THE AUTHOR'S IMAGINATION OR ARE USED FICTITIOUSLY. ANY RESEMBLANCE TO ACTUAL EVENTS, LOCALES, ORGANIZATIONS, OR PERSONS, LIVING OR DEAD, IS ENTIRELY COINCIDENTAL AND BEYOND THE INTENT OF THE AUTHOR.

# JADED

**Friends to lovers...**

Detective Roland Wright lives a lonely and solitary life, filling his waking hours with work and volunteering. It's been ten years since he lost the love of his life to a drunk driver, but he's still plagued by nightmares.

When a young man shows up at the soup kitchen where he volunteers, Roland tries to convince himself the attraction he feels is purely platonic. At least the handsome stranger is older than he looks, but can Roland risk getting close when his new friend isn't even gay?

Tyler Foster has lived on the streets since he aged out of the system. When a helpful

## EVIE RILEY

police officer from the soup kitchen gets him a job, and a real place to live, Tyler feels like life is finally giving him the break he's prayed for.

Still a virgin, Tyler is confused when he feels an attraction to the larger man. Roland is unlike anyone he's ever met and he makes Tyler feel things he doesn't understand.

When he confides in Roland about his past, the truth hits closer to home than either man could have imagined. With Roland beside him, Tyler is willing to do anything to help build the case. Together, they are determined not to let any more children suffer the same fate.

Will Roland and Tyler escape the past and find a future together?

# CHAPTER ONE

Roland

"YOU KNEW WHAT you signed up for!" The strength of my voice made the words echo off of our kitchen walls.

"I didn't sign up for this! I didn't sign up for a military life!"

"You knew I was in the military when we met, Shane. This isn't some new thing. I told you I wanted to be a Ranger

## EVIE RILEY

*and in order for that to happen I have to move to Georgia. Why can't you be supportive?"*

*"Supportive? Supportive of you going out on dangerous missions. Supportive of you getting injured or killed? How the hell am I supposed to be supportive of that? I've entertained you being in the military and humored you, because I thought it was a phase. I thought you would come to your senses and see that a life behind a desk was better for us. How the hell are we supposed to get married and have a real life together if you can't even admit that you're gay?"*

*"It's not that simple. You know that I can't just come out to the guys. If they have a problem with it, they might not have my back in the field. You said you didn't care. That it didn't bother you."*

# JADED

*"And you actually thought I would be happy to live a life hidden in the shadows forever? That I would be happy to hear the man who supposedly loves me talking about whatever imaginary girl he banged just so the guys will feel more comfortable? You promised me marriage, you promised me kids, and now you have taken all of that away. I won't be your dirty secret!"*

*"You're not, but you can't keep pressuring me like this. It's my life and I'll live it how I see fit!"*

*"Then it's a life you'll be living without me. I'm not going to be kept hidden away, and I'm not going to be left here while you are out there, never knowing if you're coming home to me."* Shane grabbed his car keys and stormed toward the door.

*"Fine, if that's how you feel I don't*

## EVIE RILEY

*need you. You can get the hell out of my life!"*

*The house shook as the front door slammed shut.*

My breath caught in my throat as I shot up in bed. My body was damp from the sweat that covered it and I could feel the tremble that threatened to overtake my whole body. This was not my first nightmare. Hell, this wasn't even the thousandth. They often plagued me and I was never lucky enough to wake up not remembering them. If it wasn't my time overseas from the war that I fought for three years, it was of my own personal hell. The night that changed everything in my life. The night I lost the most amazing man. A man that could very well have been my soulmate.

And it was all my fault.

# JADED

My own stupidity that drove him away that night.

When you are twenty-one everything in life seems so simple. I was so stupid back then, so naive to believe that I could have a military life and be gay without it ever affecting my job or my home life. I thought the best solution was to hide it, like it was some disease that I needed to keep secret.

Stupid.

So unbelievably stupid.

A quick look at the clock showed me it was just after four in the morning and I knew I wouldn't be able to get back to sleep. Letting out a sigh, I forced my sore and tired body to move. After eleven years, I had become used to functioning off little to no sleep. Being in the army for three years had started the normalcy

## EVIE RILEY

of little sleep between boot camp, training, and missions. Then my time as a New York cop solidified it. When you work as a homicide detective in a big city like New York, you get used to getting called out of bed at any hour of the evening and working two or three days straight with only bad station house coffee to keep you going.

Making my way into the bathroom, I did my best to avoid the mirror. I knew what would be looking back at me. A man with red, tired eyes that carried a haunted look in them. For the most part, I could cover up my pain, push through it and wear a mask during the day. People in this small town didn't know anything personal about me and that was how I wanted it to be.

I had only been there for four years,

## JADED

when the toll of being a homicide detective became too much. I was handling it just fine, but then the Michelle Wilson case came my way and I realized that I couldn't do it anymore.

Michelle Wilson was a beautiful four year old little girl who had been found dead in a dumpster four years ago. It wasn't just because of her age, it was because she had been raped and tortured thirty-six hours before her death.

She was never reported missing.

The investigation took me three weeks to solve. Three weeks of having to re-read the Coroner's report. Three weeks of having to see the photos of the brutal acts done to her. Three weeks of interviewing her parents who were completely devastated.

# EVIE RILEY

Three weeks for me to discover that her so-called devastated parents were actually her kidnappers.

Michelle Wilson's prints and DNA finally came back from the lab and they matched a missing two year old girl named Rebecca Watts. She had been kidnapped one night while the parents were away at dinner. She had been left with a babysitter who was killed trying to protect her. Rebecca Watts was one of thirty-six children that had been kidnapped for a child sex trafficking ring. Her death had broken the case wide open and with the help of the Feds, we were able to shut it down.

The case itself wasn't necessarily the part that broke me. It was afterward, when the whole precinct was celebrating the win. To them it was a win, but to me

# JADED

it was a great loss.

Because we had failed Rebbeca.

We had failed her parents and now they would forever be haunted by her death and what she had experienced in the last two years of her life. We had saved only ten out of the thirty-six that we knew to be out there. The other twenty-six were already sold and gone. We had lost them.

There was no win.

There was nothing to celebrate.

It was in that moment that I realized I couldn't do it anymore. So, when I saw the posting for a new detective here, I immediately applied, and given my experience in a large city, I was hired on the spot.

Now, three years later, I was trying to do what I could to keep this small town safe. There weren't really murders that happened here, but there were crimes, nonetheless. There were three gangs that ran the criminal enterprises in town, two of which were small-time and nothing to worry about too much.

Drugs were in every town and we did our best to make sure we didn't have any labs cooking them. The Draggos were the ones that caused the most violence and harm in the town. We had been working on trying to get them shut down, but with no victims willing to come forward, it had put a serious delay in the process.

At least, until six of their top guys made the mistake in attacking Devon St. James at the bus depot two months back. The whole thing was caught on video surveillance and even if it hadn't

# JADED

been, I knew Devon would have testified against them.

He had been homeless since he was seventeen, but the man always made sure to help people and keep the streets safe. The whole reason the Draggos had targeted him was because he attacked their leader as he was trying to rape a young girl in an alley close to eight months ago. For the past two months, we had finally been able to start taking down the Draggos, and soon enough, we would have them all locked up.

After relieving myself, I headed back into my bedroom to change my sweat-soaked pants, something that was almost a daily task. I changed into some clean, dry sweat pants and a hoodie before I threw on my running shoes and hit the pavement.

# EVIE RILEY

Running had never been something I was interested in, until my boot camp days. I had discovered that it was a great way for me to get my spinning thoughts in order. Whenever I felt like I needed a moment to breathe, I would go for a run and it helped me to feel better. It helped to calm my racing mind and allow me to think clearly.

I wished I had just gone for a run that night with Shane.

Maybe everything would have turned out differently if I had.

Forcing that painful thought aside, I coaxed my mind to think about things that I could control.

Like Tyler.

He was relatively new to one of the soup kitchens that I volunteer at. That same soup kitchen was where I met

# JADED

Devon for the first time, and now he had become a member of my family.

Tyler was different compared to the other homeless people I'd interacted with. To begin with, he was young. If I had to guess, he was fifteen at most. He should have been in a home and not sleeping on the streets.

I had often tried to talk with him, but he was very shy. He never looked me in the eye and whenever I was around he seemed to shrink into himself.

I was used to that reaction, though, just because of my size. I did workout. I had always been a gym guy. Even when I was sixteen I would often work out whenever I got the chance. I still do it a few days a week to keep my body in good shape. The result, though, is that I was very buff and with that, intimidation

## EVIE RILEY

always followed. Between being in the army and in the police force, my love for working out only deepened. It came in handy when I needed to intimidate a suspect, but it also meant it took victims a few minutes to get comfortable with me.

Living in a smaller town like this, I didn't have to worry too much about the victims. Everyone knew everyone, essentially, and people here all knew that despite my size I was like a teddy bear. If I could protect you, then I would. I would lay down my life for anyone in this town.

I was worried about Tyler, though, and I suspected there had been abuse in his life just by the way he reacted to me. He was afraid of me and I could tell. Anyone that saw us together could tell. I

# JADED

hated that he was afraid of me. I would never hurt him, but it was going to take time before he understood that. Before he truly one hundred percent believed that he was safe around me. It was going to take time, but I was never afraid of hard work.

My worry for Tyler had increased some over the past two months, though. I hadn't seen him at the soup kitchen and neither had Devon. I knew he had a car. How he was driving it without a license, I didn't know, but he could have easily driven off to another town.

I was hoping he hadn't left town. I would have loved to help him try and get back on his feet. Try and find a safe place for him to live. We didn't have many foster homes, but we did have some. It was why I reached out to my friend, Isaiah, in Child Protective Services. I need to know more of his story, but I also needed to know what foster home he was in hiding from so he could be put into a safe one.

What most people didn't understand about the homeless community here in town, was that they weren't all alcoholics or drug addicts. The majority of them had some type of mental illness that had been either undiagnosed, or untreated. Some were even runaways, like Devon, who had to escape an abusive situation and just could never get back on their feet.

Thankfully, Devon had managed to get back on his feet with the help of Daryl and his older brother, Zane. Devon was now going to be in the Police Academy, and I knew he was going to

# JADED

make one hell of a cop. I was looking forward to working with him and mentoring him.

Devon was safe and now it was time to make sure Tyler was. He was one of the few that I could help and I was not about to let him slip through my fingers.

# CHAPTER TWO

Roland

"ALL RIGHT, I'VE gotten the bulk of the dishes cleaned up, Martha," I said as I dried my hands off.

It was just after seven and the mass of the dinner rush had finished. I had volunteered at St. Marks Soup Kitchen for close to three years now. I often volunteered my time for various charities in town. I wanted to make sure the community and the people in it knew that they could trust me.

That I was a friendly face whenever they needed it.

I knew that people in a small town didn't hate the police as much as they seemed to in a major city like New York, but I wasn't going to kid myself into believing that everyone loved the police in town, either. Small town or not, that didn't mean people weren't judgmental or corrupt.

In fact, I often found from my dealings with other local law enforcement agencies around New York City, that those small towns had all sorts of corruption within them. To some, it might not make much sense, but to me it did.

# JADED

Who better to be corrupt than the mayor of a small town?

It wasn't like anyone would notice or suspect anything.

After all, what small town had corruption in it?

It was that novice assumption that made it possible for bad people to hurt a lot of innocent people, even if it was their pocketbook they were targeting.

"Thank you, Roland. You are so much help around here. I honestly don't know what I would do without you." Martha placed a kiss on my cheek and it warmed my heart.

Martha was the sweetest seventy-two year old you could ever meet. She was also the most fierce seventy-two year old I had ever met. She wasn't your typical grandmother. She ran ten miles three times a week, and she kept a bat next to her bed in case anyone was stupid enough to break into her house.

If you walked into her house, you would think you walked into a time warp. It was the perfect cookie cutter home from back in the fifties, right down to the ugly brown shag carpet. She kept it pristine and there was even plastic on the furniture.

She was one of a kind and she ran the show here. There were only two soup kitchens in town, there should have been more, but the officials believed two was more than enough, just like one shelter was more than enough. It wasn't enough, nowhere near it, but there was no money to be made helping the homeless. It was a sad fact, but it was a fact, nonetheless. The town was trying to

# JADED

grow.

I had been getting crap from my Captain about trying to get better control on the homeless community. Trying to get them pushed back into the shadows for when the developers come into town. Mayor Jenson was trying to win his reelection and apparently the way he was going about it was to make sure the town grew.

I wasn't against growth, but small towns survived off the mom and pop businesses that make up the town. They survived because of tourists wanting to come and see the quaint town. I wasn't sure how well it would go over to have large construction sites all over town, but it was something we would all have to deal with soon enough.

"Why don't you head home and I'll

handle the closing tonight. I can see that your hip has been bothering you tonight."

"That's very sweet of you, but I can't leave you here all alone to handle closing."

"It's not very busy tonight, there's only a few people hanging around. Go home, put your feet up, and watch your soap," I said, flashing her a warm smile.

She would cave.

I knew she would.

She loved her soap operas and she made sure to record them every day. I had even shown her how to use the DVR that she had gotten from her kids for Christmas. Once she knew how to use it, there was no stopping her. She was a recording queen with over two hundred hours of recordings to go through.

# JADED

"Oh, all right. If you're sure."

"I am. Go on and get out of here," I said, flashing her a big smile.

She gave me a grin in return and then she headed off to grab her coat and purse.

I made my way back out to the front and started to put together the last few plates that I could store in the fridge for tomorrow. Normally around eight, the place got quiet and I would close up. The sole shelter in town tended to fill up quickly, so everyone who needed a place to stay the night would flock there in the hope of getting a bed.

It could be very busy here when there was a storm. Once the shelters filled up, anyone who didn't get a bed would seek sanctuary here for as long as they could. When I had been left to close up on

## EVIE RILEY

those nights, I would try and hold off for as long as possible, especially if the weather was horrible. I hated knowing that I would have to kick people out who had nowhere to go, nowhere safe to be. I had been trying to fight with the town council about getting more shelters built so the homeless would have a safe place to be at night, but so far there was no budging them.

At the sound of footsteps, I turned to face whoever had approached the serving station. To my surprise, it was Tyler. I had been trying to find him for two months and when I finally saw him again, he had found me.

He also found me while he sported a nasty black eye. Seeing it sent a wave of anger throughout my body. He was just a kid. He didn't deserve to be hit.

# JADED

"Who the fuck hit you?"

# CHAPTER THREE

Tyler

MY HEAD WAS killing me. Over the twenty-two years of my life, I had lost count of how many times I had been punched. Of how many black eyes I'd had. My newest black eye was nothing new to me, but that didn't change the fact that it hurt like a bitch.

For the past two months, I had been

## EVIE RILEY

working for cash at a construction site. I had been working as a laborer. The grunt, essentially. For the past two months, I had been doing back breaking work, lifting fifty to a hundred pound bags and wood loads and carrying them up multiple flights of stairs and across the job site. It was very painful and even after two months my entire body was still sore and ached from it.

I was confident in myself enough to admit that I was not a big guy. I was five foot eight and only a hundred and twenty pounds. It wasn't by choice. It was just hard to get enough food to eat. I worked as many odd jobs as I could so I could afford a meal a day, and some days, I would break down and get a second meal. When I didn't have a job and the money ran out, I would try and

## JADED

hold off as long as I could before I would go to the soup kitchen to grab something.

It wasn't that I thought a soup kitchen was beneath me. It was the harsh reality slap to the face that I was, indeed, homeless. It was easier for me to pretend that I wasn't as bad off as everyone else. I had a car that I could sleep in, after all, and up until the last five months, I could still drive it around and do deliveries. I had to stop, though, when it started to act up, and with no money to spend to fix it, it was better to baby it. Now, I just used it to sleep in and I'd only move it to get closer to where my current job was.

I grew up in the foster care system. I was a foster care baby. My parents were both foster siblings and my mother got

## EVIE RILEY

pregnant when she was fourteen. They didn't want me, and their foster parents at the time didn't want them, or a baby, so all three of us got put into different homes.

I didn't know where they were, but I ended up bouncing from one home to the next for my entire childhood. Typically, infants and toddlers had a higher chance of being adopted, but no one wanted me. I was the kid who had "problems". Those problems were asthma and a learning disability. I just wasn't healthy enough for prospective adoptive parents to take a chance. The result of being born at thirty weeks, which probably accounted for a good part of my weight issue, too.

Eighteen years in the system and thirty foster homes. They were each

## JADED

different in their own way, mostly how many kids were there and the rules. But one thing they all did share in common was there were no birthdays, no holidays of any kind, no affection, no I love yous, and they never paid for anything that they didn't have to.

It was a harsh life, one that made me grow up to not rely on or trust anyone. When I wasn't being ignored, I was being beaten. I got very good at lying to my teachers whenever they asked about a new bruise.

I had learned from watching other kids what happens when you snitch. I had been abused my whole life, mentally, emotionally, and physically. I guess I could count myself lucky that I had never been violated like some of the other kids. Small miracle, in and of

# EVIE RILEY

itself.

The worst home, though, was when I was twelve. I stayed there until I was fourteen. It was me and eight other kids, and we all slept in one room on old foam mattresses on the floor. Our foster parents were Dana and Jasper Monroe.

To the public, they were good people, valuable members of society. Jasper was a cop, now a detective, and everyone thought they were saviors. They had saved all these poor unwanted children. Behind closed doors, though, they starved us, beat us, and then used us to cook, weigh, and distribute the cocaine that they were making in the basement.

Every Sunday, we would all pile into a cargo minivan and travel to other smaller towns around ours and distribute the drugs to the town's

# JADED

dealers. Whenever one of us started to get too sick from inhaling the fumes we were surrounded by for almost twenty hours a day, they would just ship us off to the next home.

The worse part is, I still see Jasper wearing his badge, walking around town like he's this great person. People have no idea what he'd done and still does to the children he and Dana took in.

Yesterday's adventure was a shit show. I got to work like normal and everything was fine. Then, at the end of the day, my boss, Armondo, came up to me with five other huge dudes and started screaming at me about stealing tools. Apparently, in the last few days there had been tools that had gone missing.

According to my boss—ex-boss—I

was the only one it could be. I was the homeless guy, so I must have stolen them to get money for alcohol or drugs. It didn't matter that I was the one with the most to lose. I was only making fifty bucks a day, but that was two hundred and fifty a week, a lot more than I would normally be making doing other jobs. The job sucked, but at least the pay was decent, to me anyway. I would never jeopardize it by stealing tools.

Armondo hadn't agreed with me and proceeded to give me a black eye while his workers held me down and grabbed all of my cash in my wallet that I had saved up.

Now, I was back to being homeless and had moved my car to a parking lot where it wouldn't be towed or destroyed. I hadn't eaten in two days, so I walked

# JADED

my sad self to St. Marks soup kitchen for a hot meal. It was later at night, though, and I wasn't too sure if there would even be a plate left.

I had debated on going there or not. I didn't like being there. I didn't like the stereotyping and assumptions that were placed on people in there. But I was starving and I knew I needed to eat something. My painful, growling stomach and the lack of food shakes really made the decision for me, in the end.

Walking in, I immediately spied Roland behind the serving counter. This weird feeling flooded my body at the mere sight of him. I didn't know what it was about him, but it happened every time I saw him. What the feeling was, I had no idea, I couldn't put a name to it

## EVIE RILEY

to identify what exactly it was that I felt, but it happened every time I went anywhere near him. It disturbed me, in a way, annoyed me, really, that anyone could make this rush of heat, fear, whatever it was, happen in such a way.

Roland was a very big man. He had muscles for days. I knew he was a cop, a detective, and would often work out. That's all I really knew about him, outside of him being gay. I had overheard him and Devon talking about it one day a few months back.

Gay people didn't bother me. I liked Devon he was a good guy. Normally, muscular men bothered me, made me feel uncomfortable, but for some reason with Devon, it never did. He was the only man who didn't make me feel intimidated by his size. Whenever I

# JADED

didn't want to be alone at night, he would sleep in the car with me. Nothing ever happened between us, I wasn't gay, but it was as close to safe as I had ever felt and probably ever would feel.

I hadn't seen Devon since the last bad storm a few months back. I hadn't been by in two months, though. Too busy with working. Part of me felt torn between hoping to see him here and hoping I didn't. If he wasn't here, that meant he might have found work and didn't need to be here. That would be good for him. He was a good man and didn't deserve a life on the streets.

Not seeing anyone else volunteering there, I made my way over to the serving station where Roland was.

He was looking down as I approached and I was happy to have a few more

## EVIE RILEY

moments to myself before I would have to talk with him. He was going to see my black eye. It wasn't like I could cover it up from people. With him being a detective, he tended to get nosy. He wanted to make sure everyone was okay, but I still couldn't figure out if it was an act or not.

After all, Jasper Monroe was his partner.

Devon seemed to think I could trust Roland, but I don't trust anyone, not even for a second. Once you trust someone, they have complete power over you, and in my experience, that kind of power was not something you ever wanted to give to someone.

"Who the fuck hit you?"

The deadly rage in his voice instantly set me on edge. For some reason, I didn't

# JADED

expect for him to ever sound like that, to ever get mad. He had always come across as an easygoing guy. To hear that level of fury, to know that it was in him, had the little boy in me curling up into a ball. I don't do yelling and I don't do conflict. Too many years of abuse programmed into my body.

I instantly looked down, shied away, and stumbled around to find the right words. Words I knew I would never be able to get right.

"Nothing... It's nothing. Just a... a door. Is there... ah, a plate left?"

I hated that I sounded like some young kid who got caught with their hand in the cookie jar, but I couldn't help it. Hopefully, he would just move on and let it go. I doubted it, but one could hope.

## EVIE RILEY

The deep sigh that escaped his lips told me exactly how unhappy with my answer he was. I knew it was a lame excuse, but I also knew I didn't owe him any explanation.

"Yeah, we got a plate."

He headed off to grab it and I didn't even bother trying to contain the sigh of relief that escaped my body. Thankfully, he was letting this go and wasn't in the mood to push. I couldn't understand why he would be so angry, though. I was just some homeless guy. I wasn't anyone special. Certainly not someone he needed to have that level of ire over. It made no sense, but I was far too tired and hungry to try and figure out why.

He walked back with a plate and handed it to me with a warm smile. I gave him a half-smile in return and

# JADED

mumbled my thanks before I headed off. I did not want to get caught in a conversation with him. I just wanted to eat and then head out.

Making my way over to a table that was empty, I sat down and started to eat. The food here wasn't too bad. I knew the one lady, Martha, cooked a great deal of it.

She was a very sweet old lady that was one hell of a cook. She would often chat about her life, her grandchildren, and some of the hoodlums that thought they could scam her. She was the definition of a badass grandmother and it was going to be a sad and dark day when she left this world.

My mouth watering and prompted by yet another growly pang from my belly, I immediately dug into the food. It was

## EVIE RILEY

some type of meatloaf. I didn't really care what it was, though. It was warm and tasted good.

As I shoveled in the meatloaf, mashed potatoes, and peas, I could feel eyes on me. I could feel *his* eyes on me. I didn't know what it was about me, but he always watched me when I was there.

At first, I thought maybe he just found me attractive, but then there didn't seem to be any fire in his eyes when he looked at me. Nothing that would lead me to believe he found me attractive. If he wasn't attracted to me, I really didn't know what his fascination was.

The only thing I could think of was that he thought I was younger than twenty-two. I did look young. I knew that. I looked sixteen, at best. I had zero

# JADED

ability to grow facial hair and I had a baby face. If I drank, I would be getting carded well into my forties. It could very well be that he thought I was underage, but so far he hadn't ever asked me about it or given any indication that he truly believed that. In the very few conversations we'd had, he'd never pried for any personal information, something I was grateful for.

That gratefulness died the moment Roland came over and sat down next to me.

I had just finished eating and was debating on if I should stick around to see if Devon would come by. The second his considerable weight hit the bench, my whole body tensed. He wasn't close enough for our bodies to touch, but he didn't leave much room for a personal bubble.

"That eye looks pretty bad. Is the pain okay? I got some over the counter stuff you could take."

I wasn't against pain medication, but I tried not to take it unless I didn't have a choice. Medications just made me feel weird, even something as simple as an Advil. They had a way of making my head a bit foggy and loopy, not something I wanted to be when I lived on the streets. Yes, my head hurt, my eye hurt, but it wasn't something I couldn't handle.

"I'm fine."

I needed him to walk away. I didn't want to be sitting next to him. I didn't want to be in the same room as him. I seriously needed to start going to the other soup kitchen. The food tended to

## JADED

be terrible and some of the people who went there were rougher, but at least I wouldn't have to worry about running into Roland.

Normally, I could adjust to another man's size at a decent rate. It wasn't always easy like it had been with Devon. Most of the time, it took a few weeks of being around a person for me to start to feel even remotely comfortable. Yet with Roland, I could not for the life of me get this weird feeling to go away. I didn't know what it was, but I didn't like it and I was starting to get sick of it.

"I saw Devon the other day. He's doing really well. He fell in love with a good guy, Daryl, and they have been living together. Devon was injured, but he made a full recovery and now he's going into the police academy."

# EVIE RILEY

It was good to hear that Devon was doing okay, that he wasn't dead and hadn't left without taking me with him. I was happy for him. He was a good man and deserved to be in love and find proper work. It wasn't all that surprising, either, that he was going into the police academy. I knew he always wanted to be in the military but his lack of a spleen kept him out of it. I didn't even think of the police academy for him. I figured with him having no spleen it would be an issue there, too.

Apparently not.

I was happy for him.

"That's good. I'm glad he got out. He deserves it."

"He's not the only one that does. Isn't there someone I could call for you? A family that you have out there that could

## JADED

help you out?"

"I don't need help."

And I didn't. I had been taking care of myself for practically my whole life. There was no one that I could call. Some could argue that I could reach out to Devon, but he got himself free from this life and I was not about to drag him down into this world again. He didn't need me to worry about. I could take care of myself. I would figure it out, eventually. I would figure out a way to get off the streets and have a small apartment to myself.

"Everyone needs help from time to time, Ty. There's no shame in that. I can help you. I can help you find a safe place to be. You could go back to school. Life isn't supposed to be this hard."

He kept his voice calm, but it did

## EVIE RILEY

nothing to calm the tightness in my body. He definitely thought I was a minor. Even if I was, there was no way I was going back to school. Me and school didn't get along. I didn't even graduate.

Teachers always told me I must have some learning disability, but what it was, specifically, they didn't know. I didn't have any foster parents that were willing to pay for the diagnosis. I didn't go to school to learn. I went because it meant I didn't have to be surrounded by abuse. Going to school was the only time I was safe from being hit.

I wasn't popular in school. The exact opposite. People thought I was stupid. They thought I was weird. They didn't like that I was a foster kid or poor. There was always something about me that someone didn't like. But they never put

# JADED

their hands on me so it was better to listen to their words than to be at home nursing another bruise.

"It's getting late. I need to get back," I said, and stood.

I wasn't going to sit here any longer. Devon wasn't going to show, and that was good, because he would demand to know who hit me and be looking for payback. He was getting his life on track. He didn't need to deal with any drama coming from me. I didn't want to be alone in my car just yet, but it was better than feeling uncomfortable under Roland's glances.

"You got a safe place tonight?" Roland asked as he followed me toward the door.

This man never seemed to want to give up.

# EVIE RILEY

"Always." And with that, I was out the door and headed off down the street at a brisk trot to get to my car.

I couldn't figure out what Roland's deal was with me. I understood that he was a cop, but every other cop in town held no interest in helping any of the homeless. They were all too happy to arrest us and throw away the key.

So what was Roland's deal?

Why did he always look at me like that?

Why did he care what happened to me and if I had anyone or anywhere else to be?

Even if he believed I was underage, that shouldn't be enough for him to act this way. He had to want something from me. Everyone wants something from everyone. I just couldn't figure out

# JADED

what that could be, but I had a feeling my life could depend on figuring that out.

Arriving at my car, I was pleased to see that it was still there and wasn't damaged. After using the key to unlock the back, I crawled in and lay down. I had the back seat down flat so I had a bit more room.

Some people had asked me how a homeless guy could have a car, even a piece of shit like mine. When I aged out of the system, I got some money to help me get on my feet. It was supposed to be enough to get me through a month or two for rent until I was able to secure a job or if I was lucky enough go to College.

I had really looked forward to that money I'd been told I'd get. On the really rough nights, I would dream of having my own place where there was no yelling or violence. A place where I had full control.

Only, on my eighteenth birthday when I got the check, I discovered that the amount was far from what I expected. I hadn't expected a lot. I knew the system sucked and there were an endless number of flaws. But I had expected something like five thousand dollars, or twenty-five hundred. Something that would allow a person to pay first and last month's rent.

Instead, what I got was eighteen hundred dollars.

The system paid out one hundred dollars for every year I was in foster care. A hundred bucks a year to make up for all of the abuse, for the hell that I had

## JADED

been put through.

It was just another slap in the face.

I couldn't find a place to rent for that money. Not to mention, no one told me that I wouldn't be able to rent an apartment without a job, or that I couldn't get a decent job to pay for that apartment without a home address.

It was a catch twenty-two, so I did the only thing I could think of.

I bought a shitty car for a thousand bucks and saved the eight hundred to use for gas while I worked various delivery jobs and other odd jobs that I could. I still hadn't made enough to get my own place and now I was completely broke once again.

I angrily wiped the traitorous tear that ran down my cheek. I wasn't going to cry. Crying never solved anything and

## EVIE RILEY

it sure as hell never made me feel better. I had been in this position before and I would get myself out of it. I didn't need anyone. I could make it through this world all on my own, and that's exactly what I was going to do.

# CHAPTER FOUR

Roland

IT WAS JUST after nine by the time I walked back into my home. The deafening silence always hit me hard. Even after all of this time, I still expected to find Shane in the kitchen or curled up on the couch watching some romance movie. The loss of him was still fresh, even though it shouldn't be. After just

## EVIE RILEY

over a decade, one would think I would be over what happened, but I wasn't. It's always there, right below the surface, threatening to break through and pull me under.

It wasn't healthy, I knew that, but knowing it and accepting it are two very different things. I was perfectly fine just where I was. I didn't need to be fixed.

I didn't *want* to be fixed.

The ringing of my cell phone split the silence. I dug it out of my pocket as I made my way to my fridge to grab a beer. I wasn't much of a drinker, but I could use a drink tonight.

"Wright."

"Evening, Roland. Do you have a minute to chat?" Isaiah's voice had my mind shifting away from my past trauma to a current problem that I could

## JADED

potentially solve.

"Hey, Isaiah. Of course I do." I opened the beer as I made my way over to the couch and sat down as he spoke.

"So, I've managed to track down your Tyler from St. Marks. It wasn't easy with just a first name and description, but I managed to pull it out. Now, I can't legally tell you everything in his file."

"I know you can't and I'm not asking you to. I just need to know the basics so I can try and find him a safe foster home to be placed in."

"That's the thing... He's not fifteen, he's twenty-two."

*Wait, what?*

*No way.*

There was just no way. He couldn't be twenty-two. I didn't know if he was fifteen for sure, but he looked between fourteen and sixteen. There had to be a mistake. He just couldn't be twenty-two.

"That's not possible, man. You must have gotten the wrong name. There's no way he's older than sixteen. If you saw him, you would agree."

"It's your guy. He's been blessed, or cursed, with a baby face. Full name is Tyler Foster, and, before you ask, no, that's not a coincidence. He was born in the foster system and both parents didn't want him. Protocol is to give the baby a generic last name. Sometimes it's the street name that the parents were living on or the street name of the first foster home. The last name that the nurses give the baby as an ID in the hospital. He is twenty-two and nothing in his file since he aged out. I did run a security check and he hasn't been

# JADED

arrested. Most likely, he has been homeless since he aged out."

This was not what I was expecting at all. I thought it was bad when I thought he was fifteen, but to know that he had spent his whole life in the system and was now homeless, that made it worse.

"I thought kids who age out get money to get their own place for a couple of months."

"Yes, every child gets paid on their eighteenth birthday when they are kicked out of the system. Good foster parents will allow the child to stay there until they get on their feet, others toss them out that morning. What people outside of CPS don't know, though, the amount that a young adult gets when they age out is based on the number of years you have spent in the system. You are awarded one hundred dollars for every year you are in the system."

"A hundred bucks? That's it? How the hell are any of them supposed to survive on their own with eighteen hundred max?"

That was bullshit.

We were all told that children who aged out got enough money to support themselves for two months, three max if they were able to find a cheap enough place. But eighteen hundred was nothing. Most places were a thousand bucks for the first month. They wouldn't have enough to cover first and last month's rent, assuming they found a place that took them without a job. I thought the foster system was built solely to help kids, to protect them from their parents, if they needed it. They

# JADED

shouldn't get screwed over yet again when the time came for them to face this world alone.

"It's not much, I agree. It's a problem with the system that is on a Government level. On a regional level, if there was enough support for it, you could increase the amount, but that would require a lot of political and local support. We don't have that. Most people want to believe everything is fine in our quaint town, but the foster system is still the foster system, I'm afraid. Tyler has been through quite a large number of homes, but that isn't uncommon. Unfortunately, though, I can't place him in a foster home. It's on him to try and get a steady job and secure an apartment."

"Yeah, okay. Thanks, man. I'll see

what I can do for him. At least now I know there isn't a family out there looking for him."

"I wish there was more that I could do for him. He's had a hard life, Roland. Be careful with him. He won't trust easily."

"I will," I promised before I ended the call.

I could tell that Tyler had been through some hard times, that was made very clear by his demeanor toward me. I wasn't stupid. I had eyes. He was unsettled by me and my size. I hated it, but I couldn't fix his natural reaction to me. It'd been happening since I was eighteen, I was used to people finding me intimidating, but it still hurt to know that Tyler was a bit scared of me. I was going to have to work my ass off to start building any semblance of trust with

## JADED

him.

There was one other emotion that ran through me at hearing that Tyler was in fact twenty-two. Relief. I wish I could say it was because that would mean a child wasn't living on the streets, but it wasn't. I was relieved because I'd been feeling a slight attraction to Tyler. Yes, he was smaller than I normally went with, he looked young, not to mention the skittish behavior. Tyler is what I would call man pretty with his soft features and lack of facial hair. I tended to go with larger guys that were full of confidence and were more rugged looking.

However, every now and then when I was able to catch his gaze, I couldn't help but notice how beautiful his eyes were. He had amazing blue eyes that pulled you in. I could get lost in them easily, and that wasn't something I was used to. He was the exact opposite of what I normally found attractive, but he was haunting my thoughts and even my dreams. It was a huge relief to know that I wasn't some pervert finding a kid attractive.

Knowing he wasn't a minor didn't make things any easier, though. I still had to earn his trust. I still needed to try and help him get off the street, something that would not be easy. I could offer a hand out to him, but it was all up to him to take the offered hand. I was hoping he would.

As for my attraction to him, I didn't even know if he was gay. I wasn't going to put him in that position. He needed a friend. He needed someone on his side

## JADED

and that was exactly what I was going to be. If him being gay came out down the road, I could reevaluate then.

Taking a drink from the amber-colored bottle, I grabbed the remote and started to flip through the channels, looking for a hockey game to watch. I wasn't going to sleep anytime soon, so I might as well try to turn my mind off.

The last thing I needed to do right now was continue thinking about Tyler.

# CHAPTER FIVE

Roland

AFTER DROPPING OFF my jacket at my desk, I made my way into the break room at work. The station wasn't very big, especially compared to what I had been used to out in New York.

The station I worked out of in New York, had been eight floors, with multiple break rooms on each floor.

# EVIE RILEY

There were ten different units within the station and all of them were detective units.

Here, though, it was half of the size of one floor in my old station. The whole building was roughly a thousand square feet and it held four detectives, myself included, the twelve patrol officers, and my Captain. There wasn't any elbow room and often no coffee, but the cases that I worked were a hell of a lot easier on my mind than any case that came across my desk in New York.

"Can you believe they actually let a fag into the academy?" Baxter's voice traveled down the short hallway.

His words instantly had my whole body on edge. It wasn't necessarily just his words. I knew that most people in town still didn't accept or like

## JADED

homosexuals and the police force was no different. I'd come across problems in New York when I decided to come out. That was after Shane. My fear of not being accepted had put him in that car that night, I wasn't going to make the same mistake twice. It was who he was talking about. I knew there was only one new cadet within the police academy that was gay.

*Devon.*

While Devon had been healing from his attack, I'd made a point of going by to see him once a day whether he was in the hospital or not. One day we got to talking and I discovered he had wanted to be in the Rangers, but his lack of a spleen, thanks to his asshole of a father, had cost him that dream.

I had suggested he could be a cop,

even without a spleen. As long as he took vitamins to help with his immune system and saw a doctor to prescribe him a coagulant to ensure he wouldn't bleed out from an attack.

I was very pleased and happy for him when he told me he had been accepted into the academy. That was a month ago, and he'd started a week ago in the academy.

I had been checking in on him and the instructors all said he was a natural, especially his marksmanship. They were already talking about training him on being a sharpshooter, should we ever need a sniper. I doubted we ever would. This town wasn't one that had hostage situations or even the need for a police raid. Still, I couldn't have been more proud of him.

# JADED

"I heard he was good," Jarod commented.

"He's probably sucking their cocks to give him a decent mark. This is what we're letting to happen to our station? We're going to let fags and homeless people in? He's going to be too busy staring at our asses and daydreaming about our dicks to be doing any work," Baxter said snidely, letting out a chuckle just as I walked in the room.

See, in my option this is where a smart man would look down and shuffle out of the room. They both knew I was gay and they both knew I was the one that helped Devon get into the academy and saw him often. They knew this, and yet Baxter just smirked at me as Jarod started to shuffle slowly toward the door.

"You know what I'm talking about,

# EVIE RILEY

Wright. You're from the big city. You know what homeless people are really like. They're all messed up with different mental illnesses, not to mention lazy drunks or junkies. We can't have someone like that wearing the uniform. Besides, we already got our residential queer with you here," Baxter said with a smirk.

My hands balled into fists as I tried to push down the anger. Normally, I would do one of two things: walk away and just ignore the ignorance, or I would put him in his place with a verbal lashing. I did out rank him and often it wasn't worth the effort to try and change his opinions about homosexuality.

Maybe it was the lack of sleep over the past few years.

Maybe it was from learning more

# JADED

about Tyler.

Maybe it was because I knew Devon and what he had been through with his father.

Whatever it was, I lost it. I threw a punch, catching him right in his jaw, and knocked him flat on his ass. The sound of the coffee mug in his hand shattering on the ground and him falling into the cart on his way down was enough to catch the attention of everyone in the building. Everyone including my Captain, who stormed in just as I was considering punching Baxter again as he sat there dazed on the ground, coffee from his broken mug slowly working its way over to his pants.

"What the fuck is going on in here!" Captain Perry demanded.

"I punched Baxter," I easily admitted.

## EVIE RILEY

I was man enough to own up to my actions and decisions. Plus, it was pretty clear that it was only me, Baxter, and Jarod in the room. We all knew Jarod wasn't going to be punching anyone. He was more quiet and timid. He was the guy that went along to get along.

"Get your ass in my office now, Detective Wright!"

Captain Perry stormed out of the room and I looked down at Baxter, as Jarod, who'd finally snapped out of his daze, helped him up. I should have felt bad for punching a fellow officer, but I didn't. He deserved it and maybe now he would think twice before he started to mouth off.

Turning on my heel, I strolled out of the break room and made the short walk down to my Captain's office. I closed the

# JADED

door, not that it would matter if he started to yell. Giving him my full attention, I started to explain myself.

"Sir, if you knew what Baxter was saying..."

"I don't give two shits if he told you he slept with your wife," Captain Perry cut me off, but before he could continue, I cut him off.

"Husband, sir. If I had a spouse, it wouldn't be a wife, but a husband. Which you know, because I told you in my interview that I was gay and wouldn't entertain accepting your offer if that was going to be a problem for you or anyone within your force. I've been dealing with Baxter's crap for years. I've been listening to his little snide comments about gay people for years. Today was the first day that I've hit him and he had it coming."

I didn't hide that I was gay and I'd finally had enough. I wasn't going to continue to deal with hearing those nasty little homophobic comments all the time. If I ever did find a man to fall in love with one day, I wanted to be able to bring him to my work. I wanted to be able to hold his hand in public without having to deal with any comments or looks about it from the men that are supposed to be my brothers, supposed to have my back. It was time everyone knew I wasn't going to tolerate it any longer.

"I have no problem with you being gay, Wright. I told you that from the jump. But that doesn't mean you get to knock out another member of this department. You think I don't know that

## JADED

Baxter is an asshole? His daddy was one, too. Yep, same as his daddy. He's a tenth generation asshole, but that doesn't give you the right to hit a subordinate. What the hell is going on with you?"

Gone was the harsh tone and it was instantly replaced with a softer one. It always amazed me how he could go from one high emotion to the next within seconds. He could get to a boiling rage and then flip a switch without any effort.

I didn't know much about Captain Perry, but I knew he was from out west, California, and had seen his fair share of trauma in his time. I suspected it was one of the reasons why he picked me for this job. He understood my need to get out of a big city.

"Nothing. I'm fine."

# EVIE RILEY

"Bullshit you are. You think I haven't noticed how you've been going downhill over the past three years since you got here. I thought that haunted look in your eyes would dissipate after you had some time to recover from the traumas you have gone through, but instead it has only gotten worse. You're not sleeping, you're working even when you are off duty, you're no longer social, and now you are punching people. You've left me with no choice, Wright. I'm suspending you."

"What? You can't suspend me!"

This couldn't happen.

He couldn't suspend me.

I'd never been suspended in my entire adult career. I didn't have black marks on my record. I'd always made sure to do my job to the best of my ability and I

# JADED

respected the Upper Brass. I needed to work. I needed to keep busy. I couldn't be stuck in my house with nothing but my own thoughts to keep me company.

"You punched a subordinate in my station. You're damn right I can suspend you. I could suspend you for a month in accordance with the regulations. But I'm not about to bench my best detective, small town or not. The length of your suspension is completely up to you. All you have to do is provide me with a signed note from a licensed therapist that says you went and spoke with them."

"You want me to do what?"

A therapist.

*Ah, hell no.*

I wasn't going to talk to some shrink who would only turn around and tell me

## EVIE RILEY

I was crazy and shouldn't be allowed to carry a gun. That wasn't going to happen.

"You need to see a shrink. It's time, Roland. I don't know what you have been through. I can make assumptions based on what I've been through, but I know that my traumas are not the same as yours. I struggled for many years before I moved here. It cost me my wife of twenty years and my two children, who still, to this day, refuse to take my calls. By the time I went and saw Dr. Alex Howard, I had lost everything. I don't want that for you. And I don't want you worried that you are going to lose your job because you are seeing a therapist. You're not, no matter what they say. I know you can do this job and you are the only person within this

# JADED

department that I know without a doubt can handle pretty much any damn situation that comes up. This is about your mental health and that is just as important as your physical health."

I swallowed around the lump that had formed in my throat. I had no idea he had seen a shrink. A local shrink. I just figured he was like every other cop, you push the erase button and override the memories. You bury it down deep inside of you and move on. That's how you are taught in the military and in the police academy. It's how I'd always operated and now he wanted me to open all of these boxes of horror.

My knee jerk reaction was *hell no.*

It wasn't going to happen.

He would cave eventually.

The problem was, he wouldn't. He

## EVIE RILEY

wouldn't cave, because he believed one hundred percent that I needed to do this. Rationally, I knew he was just looking out for me, but irrationally, it felt like he was out to get me.

"See Dr. Howard, or see someone else in town, I don't care. But if you want to come back to work, you need a session completion form signed and given to me. And you need to do that every time you go, twice a week, for the next few months. After three months, it'll be up to you if you wish to continue. Mandatory, twice a week for ninety days. You've gone to war four times, Roland. You've faced gunshots, knives, bombs, terrorists, and everything in between. You can face a therapist. I believe in you and I will always be there for you, no matter the time of day or night."

## JADED

I didn't want to hear this. I didn't want to hear any of this, especially in his soft and understanding tone. Life was easier if I kept people at a distance. Even Zane, Daryl, and Devon. I was friendly with them and I had no problem talking to them if they had a problem. But I kept my personal life private.

Talking about my time overseas, as an NYPD Detective, Shane, it made my chest tight. I didn't want to talk about it. I didn't want to hear the words that I had been dreading. Words that I had thought myself in the quiet of the night.

That I had PTSD.

Logically, I knew it wasn't a terminal illness. Lots of cops and soldiers have it and operate perfectly fine in the field. The home life could be a little off, but it was something they could live with. That didn't make it any less terrifying, though, and I had been doing everything within my power to convince myself that I didn't have it.

That the nightmares were nothing.

That the bouts of depression and anti-social behavior were normal.

That any insomnia was just because of work and my mind was busy working out a case.

Sitting down with a therapist could make it all real. It could cement what my mind had been trying to tell me for years and that absolutely terrified me.

"Couldn't we just compromise and I take a week off?" I tried. I had to try and at least bargain with him.

He gave me a warm smile that did nothing to remove the cold that had seeped into my bones.

# JADED

"No, but you can go and see someone tomorrow and come back to work right afterward, if you want. And no one will know that you are suspended. I'll tell them you are on a special assignment for me. This stays between us. You can do this, Roland, I know you can. And I promise, you will be happy that you did one day. I know it might not seem like it, but you will be."

That wasn't going to happen. I was being given a prison sentence of ninety days and I was going to hate every second I was stuck in that shrink's office. At least it was only two hours a week. A grand total of a hundred and eighty hours. I knew I would be keeping a mental calculator in my head and counting down until I was finally free.

This was going to be the longest three

months of my life.

"Don't be holding your breath for that. I guess I'll see you tomorrow."

I didn't wait for his reply. It didn't matter right now, anyway. He knew I wasn't happy about this and he accepted that. I made my way out of the station and made sure to not make eye contact with anyone. I needed to get out of here. I needed to work these emotions off.

*The gym.*

Yes, I needed the gym, but first I had to head home to get changed and lock my gun up. I just needed to keep busy until I could get this over and done with.

## CHAPTER SIX

Tyler

THE HEAT WAS starting to get to me today. It was always hard during the warmer spring and summer months for my asthma. The result was more asthma attacks that required me to use my inhaler more frequently. Today, I had to get a refill, which is why I was stuck out in the hot sun standing outside of a free

## EVIE RILEY

clinic waiting for my turn.

Why was I outside?

Because the waiting room was full of other patients. All twenty of them. You wouldn't think in a town this size that there would be much of a wait for a free clinic, but it was always busy and under staffed.

The doctors didn't want to work here, because they wanted to make real money. But the doctors that were in town had to volunteer here so many hours a month to keep a discount on their malpractice insurance, so they grudgingly did what they had to for a few bucks back in their pocket.

They often didn't care too much about the non-paying patients they had to see. The whole process was basically the same. You go, sign your name on a

# JADED

clipboard, wait to be called, get called, wait even longer in the room. When the doctor does finally appear, they get your name wrong, they only listen for a minute before they either give you a drug you might not have needed or they tell you that you're fine when you really aren't. If you were actually paying, you wouldn't be able to get out of the room because the doctor would talk your ear off. It was complete crap, but it was another piece of my reality.

At least today I just needed a refill, so hopefully, it wouldn't be too much of an issue. I was only allowed to have one cartridge at a time. Apparently, they were worried I could be selling it to someone. Even if I could find someone that would pay me for it, why would they buy it?

## EVIE RILEY

It's not like steroids could make them high and it wasn't a pill that they could crush up to snort or inject. It was annoying, because sometimes a single cartridge could last me a month or longer, but sometimes it only lasted me two weeks if we were in a heat wave and I was working outside. The past two months, I'd been using it a lot while working outside at the construction site.

Feeling a little light headed, I went and sat down on the ground with my back against the bricks. I wished there was some shade, but there was nothing around me that I could use to get some relief from this heat.

I wasn't the only one out here in this heat, there were four other guys waiting in line ahead of me. They were all waiting for their methadone. I wasn't

# JADED

judging, but I had seen them around quite a bit and I could see the signs of withdrawals starting to creep in on them. I also knew that before they even got in there, they would be getting worse and starting to get aggressive until they got their fix.

Letting out a small sigh I bent my knees up and placed my head in my hands to try and push through the tightness in my chest.

"Tyler?"

*This isn't happening.*

How is it he was always around when I felt like complete crap?

It was like he had some type of radar or something. Slowly lifting my head and squinting in the harsh sunlight as I looked his way, I spoke.

"Detective."

# EVIE RILEY

Roland moved so he blocked the sun with his enormous body before he bent down in front of me, still managing to block out the sun.

"Are you okay?" he asked in a caring voice as his eyes scanned over the parts of my body that he could see. "Is your eye bothering you?"

"It's fine. I need a refill," I said as I held up my inhaler slightly while also managing to look away.

That feeling was back. What was it about him?

"You have asthma. It must be pretty bad in this heat. They need to listen to your lungs, I'd imagine."

His concern for me was confusing. I wasn't really used to someone being concerned for me. I didn't understand why he would be worried or concerned

# JADED

for my welfare. I was just some homeless guy. I wasn't anything special.

"I'm waiting to get my refill. I have to wait for a doctor to give it to me."

They wouldn't listen to my lungs. The doctor wouldn't even be bothered to know my name. That was just fine with me. I had my share of doctors growing up.

"Can I see that for a second?" he asked with a nod at my inhaler.

I wasn't sure why he wanted to see it, but it wasn't like he could do anything to damage it. I doubted he would run away with it. I held it up for him and he easily took it and popped the cartridge out.

"Yeah, I thought so. You see this red diamond by the prescription name?" he asked, turning it back to me so I could see it. I gave a slight nod before he continued. "Any prescription with that mark lets pharmacists know that it is safe to be refilled without a prescription. You don't have to wait for a prescription from a doctor, you just go into any pharmacy and they will give you your refill." He handed it back to me as I spoke.

"Wait, are you serious?"

I didn't have to wait?

I could actually go into a pharmacy and just hand my inhaler over and they would give me my refill, just like that?

If that was true, then why didn't any doctor ever tell me that?

Every month for the past four years I'd had to wait in line to see a doctor. I'd had to go through this dance every time I needed a refill. I had to wait hours just to be treated like a nuisance because I

## JADED

needed medication for my lungs. It always made me feel like I was being a burden or bothersome to them. Like it was my fault that I had asthma, like I had done something wrong and this was the end result.

It always felt like I was the problem child. I was always made to feel like I was causing problems with my health. I was born premature and that came with health problems. Problems that I had to live with for the rest of my life. Thankfully, the worst of it was my asthma, but that brought other problems with it. I had to be really careful not to get any chest infections because it would be made worse with my asthma. I'd had a hard time with my weight and getting up to an average level. All I had to do was eat a healthy diet and often, but that didn't work with life on the streets.

"Yes. I don't know how long you've had to be on an inhaler and why no doctor has ever told you. But you just need to go into a pharmacy and they'll take care of it for you."

Unbelievable.

This whole time I could have just done that. This is what people don't seem to understand. People who are homeless are treated like we're less than the dirt everyone walks on. We're an annoyance, an inconvenience, and no one holds any interest in helping or making things a bit easier on us. All it would have taken was one doctor or even a nurse to open their mouth and tell me and then they could have never seen me again.

## JADED

Why have to go through this whole process as a doctor if you could have avoided it by just informing me of something this simple?

It was ridiculous and not something that I would have had to go through if I wasn't at a free clinic. They would have had no problem if I was paying, but I wasn't paying so I was going to get the least amount of effort they could provide. Like I wasn't a human being just trying to survive like everyone else.

"Thanks." Letting out a sigh, I stood up. There was a pharmacy not too far from here. Hopefully, they would fill it without giving me any problems. The last thing I wanted to do was to have to be at the back of the line.

"I'll walk with you. Make sure they don't try and give you the runaround,"

## EVIE RILEY

he offered, but I could tell it wasn't a suggestion.

I wanted to argue that it wasn't necessary, but I truly didn't know if it wouldn't be. At least if he was with me, I wouldn't have to worry about the Pharmacist giving me a hard time and denying my request.

I simply gave a nod and we headed down the street for the short walk. He didn't talk and for that I was thankful. I wasn't sure what I would even say at this point. He still believed I was underage and I wasn't in a real hurry to correct his assumption. It wasn't anyone's business how old I was, especially a cop. If he thought I was underage, then he wouldn't be trying to arrest me for some bullshit excuse. There was a safety in being perceived as

# JADED

young to the police.

Arriving at the pharmacy, we immediately headed back to where the prescription counter was. After a quick explanation, the Pharmacist had no problem giving me my refill. I still couldn't believe how easy it was to get it. I expected to have to argue with them and then inevitably have to go back to wait in an even longer line at the free clinic. The whole task took seven minutes and then we were back outside on the sidewalk.

"Thank you for this. I really appreciate it," I said, a small smile turning up the corners of my lips.

"It's no problem at all. There's something I wanted to talk to you about. Why don't we grab some food at the diner? My treat."

## EVIE RILEY

Going anywhere with him didn't seem like a good idea. That odd feeling was only getting stronger when I was around him and I still didn't know what it was.

At the same time, if he wanted to talk to me about something, could I really say no?

I didn't know what he wanted to talk about but if it had anything to do with him suspecting I did something illegal, it would be better to get it sorted out early before it grew into a monster.

Plus, I hadn't eaten since dinner at the soup kitchen, how could I turn down free food?

"Okay," I said, but I couldn't hide the uncertainty in my voice.

He simply gave me a warm smile and started to walk down the street toward the diner. I wasn't too sure about this,

## JADED

but my feet seemed to move all on their own and I followed.

He didn't say anything again and I couldn't help but wonder if he was a man of few words or was just terrible at small talk. Either way was fine with me. It wasn't like we were friends and I didn't hold any interest in filling the silence with pointless conversation.

As we approached the diner, I couldn't help but wonder if maybe Devon would be working. I knew he was going to be a police officer, but I wasn't sure if he was still working at the same time. A quick scan when we walked in told me he wasn't there. We sat down at a booth off to the left side of the building as one of the female servers brought our menus to us.

"Do you have a go-to diner food?"

## EVIE RILEY

Roland asked, after we placed our drink orders.

"I've never eaten in a diner before, so I'll go with no."

Diners and restaurants were a no go growing up and especially after being homeless for four years now. Whenever I got food, I always tried to make sure it was something that could last a few days. Going out to eat was a waste of money to me, because it was money I could use to get food for a few days, as opposed to a single meal.

"The food here is really good. I'm a burger guy myself."

I liked burgers, but my body had a hard time processing that much protein in one sitting. It always left me feeling heavy and that wasn't a good feeling to have when living on the street. The

# JADED

omelets looked good, though. At least the photos of them did.

The words got all mixed up in my head so I just ignored them. I didn't normally get breakfast food. When the waitress came back over with our drinks we both placed our order before she walked off with a warm smile.

"The omelets are really good here. I'm a big breakfast guy, it's the most important meal of the day, but I like eggs and hash browns. Sometimes I'll make it for dinner."

"I used to cook it a lot. It's cheap to feed multiple people."

"While you were in the foster homes?" he asked, gently.

It was a logical assumption that I had been in foster homes, but the look in his eyes told me it was more than just an assumption. He was a cop, so he could easily have tried to find a file on me. I had never been arrested, but in the system was in the system. It was all the same, especially in a town like this.

"You pulled my file," I easily stated, as I sat back. I wasn't mad. I wasn't anything. I had accepted that the police in this town would do whatever they wanted. All you could do was hope you didn't get on their bad side.

"No, no. I called my friend in Social Services and he was able to find your file. I don't know much of any of it, actually. He would never betray anyone like that. He just told me that you were in the foster system since you were born and that you were twenty-two. Now, before you get upset, I only started trying to find information on you

## JADED

because I believed you were fifteen or so. I never would have done it had I known you were of legal age."

I believed him.

For some reason, I actually believed him. He didn't intend to invade my privacy. He had done it with good intentions and I couldn't fault him for that. I looked young and as a cop he'd decided to try and make sure I was safe and off of the streets. I could respect that.

"It's okay, and yeah, once you start becoming the oldest it's on you to take care of the kids. A dozen eggs and a bag of potatoes can feed six kids for a few days," I said with a small shrug.

"Not much food for that many kids," he said as his brows crinkled slightly.

I could understand his point. It

## EVIE RILEY

wasn't much food. And often, I would go a few days without eating just so the younger kids would get something each day. It was hard, especially when I had to tell one of them that they couldn't have more. I made it work, though, because it wasn't their fault. They didn't ask for it any more than I did, but I could at least give them some semblance of safety and care.

"The foster system is far from sunshine and rainbows. The kids all work together to do what they can to survive."

"And you haven't been able to get on your feet since you aged out?"

"The small amount that I got for aging out wasn't much. It wasn't enough to cover first and last month's rent for a deposit. The places that I could afford to

## JADED

rent, they wouldn't take me because I didn't have a job and no one was willing to give me the chance to find one while living there, either. I bought my car and now I live in it. I've been trying to work wherever I can, but most places want an address and I can't give them one."

"I agree with you on that completely." He shook his head as he spoke. "It's insane how people treat those that are homeless. I know a lot of great guys that have been struggling and trying to get on their feet, but no one will rent to them without a job, but they can't get a job without having a home. No one seems to want to help. I've been trying to help where I can, but I also know as a cop I can be off putting because of that."

"Not a lot of people trust cops, especially in this town. Plus, physically, you don't help yourself."

He was making me nervous and we were just sitting here. I knew it wasn't his fault, though. It was mine from my own traumas. But I also knew I wasn't the only one with those kind of traumas within the homeless community.

"I know. I have this unique ability to clear a room by just walking into it." He chuckled. "I never used to be this size. I was actually closer to yours when I was younger. But I joined the military and that started me on a strict training schedule. It stuck with me."

I wasn't all that surprised that he used to be in the military. His very slight accent told me he was from the New York area. Someone his size and with his accent, it made sense that he was military.

## JADED

Most likely the Army in one of the divisions.

It also made a lot of sense why him and Devon hit it off right away. Devon had always wanted to be a Ranger before his abusive father ripped that away from him.

The waitress was back with our food and at the delicious smell of it my stomach growled. The food looked even better than it did in the photos and the smell was to die for.

"I don't know if you are interested, but my friend, Oswald, he's got a bar and he's looking for a bartender. He's been having a hard time trying to get someone that actually wants to work. Now, it's a dive bar so it's not fancy. Most people just do a beer and a shot, and the people that go there are blue-

## EVIE RILEY

collar workers. But if you're okay with that, I could set up a meeting for you and him to sit and talk it over."

"Are you serious?"

Was he actually going to give me the chance to get a stable job?

I had never bartended before, but if it was just a beer or a shot, I could do that. I wouldn't be very good at fancy drinks, but I could handle basic bartending. If I could meet with someone and have the chance to convince them that I would be a good fit, that could be exactly what I needed to start getting back on my feet.

"Absolutely. He's a great guy. I met him when I first moved here. I've been going to his bar since day one. It's a small and old building, so the bar isn't anything to rave about in terms of decor.

# JADED

And the majority of the customers, like I said, are all construction workers and low income people. There are also only four servers, two on each shift and one bartender a shift. So it can get busy, but the tips are decent, from what the girls have said."

I didn't care what the bar looked like or how busy it would be. It was a chance to have an actual steady job. That was the only thing I cared about. I didn't care what I had to do if it meant I could have the chance to actually get a place to live and make steady money.

"If you want to set something up I would appreciate it. I've never done any bartending before, but I'm a quick learner."

I was a quick learner if it was away from books. Working with my hands and

## EVIE RILEY

following a routine was something I excelled at. If I could meet with his friend, maybe I could convince him to give me a chance.

"I don't doubt that. I'll set it up for you. He'll be happy, I'm sure of it. He hasn't been able to find anyone and he's been working doubles for a couple of weeks now. I'll call him later and get a time for you. I'll be at the Soup Kitchen tomorrow night, so if you swing by, I can let you know the details."

I easily agreed. I wasn't planning on going to St. Mark's for a couple of days, but I would if that meant I could have a potential interview. Today had turned out a lot differently than I had expected. I thought I would be stuck in a line up for the day, only to now have the chance to have a real job. If Roland was able to

## JADED

get me a meeting with his friend, I would make sure I did everything I could to secure that job and keep it.

This opportunity could be the very thing I needed to have a real chance at a true life and I was not about to let that slip through my fingers.

# CHAPTER SEVEN

Roland

THIS WAS STUPID and completely unnecessary. Baxter was being an asshole and deserved to be laid out for the crap he was spewing. If it had been anyone else, I doubted that Captain Perry would be forcing them to speak to a shrink over it.

*Damn it.*

## EVIE RILEY

I was fine.

I didn't need this.

So what if I had nightmares every night?

So what if I didn't sleep some nights?

So what if there have been moments where I could swear I've seen or heard him?

I was fine.

I didn't have a problem.

I didn't need to be fixed.

There was nothing wrong with me.

*Ugh.*

I was going to this appointment and then I would be back at work tomorrow. The fact that I had to do this for three months was complete shit, but if I wanted to keep my job, I had no choice.

Walking into the office had me feeling a mixture of emotions. The first was

# JADED

shame. Dr. Howard's office was the only one in this building so the receptionist would know I was here for him and anyone that saw me outside would know I was here for him as well.

People knowing my personal information made me feel uncomfortable. Like I was on display at some freak show and everyone paid ten bucks to see the show.

As a cop, I had referred many victims to speak to a therapist in the past. Easily over three hundred victims I had introduced to a therapist, someone that could help them overcome the trauma that they had endured. Never, not once, had I ever thought less of them or told them that they should be ashamed. Yet, as I walked through the door it was all I could feel.

## EVIE RILEY

I couldn't help but wonder if they felt the same way as well. If they thought I was a liar because I told them it would be fine. Because I told them they had nothing to be ashamed of when that might have been all they felt.

This was ridiculous.

I wasn't a victim.

I had been through some hard shit in my life, yes, but I survived and I was one of the lucky ones that got to keep living. I didn't feel very lucky sometimes, but that is what everyone always said when you survived a tour. You were one of the lucky ones because you didn't get shot, blown up, or tortured while you were off fighting for your country. A country that was made up of thousands upon thousands of people that didn't appreciate it and assumed you were just

## JADED

a paid government assassin.

Pushing back some of the bad memories from my time overseas that were banging on my mental door, I turned my attention to the office. It was warm and welcoming with a rich brown paint on the walls and pieces of local artwork hung up. There were a few couches that made up the waiting room.

With the town being on the smaller side, it allowed for doctor offices to be more intimate with nicer furniture compared to plastic chairs that you typically found in larger cities. It was designed to be welcoming and to put you at ease, but it had the opposite effect on me.

I wanted to run from the building.

I wanted to lie to the receptionist about why I was here. I would have

# EVIE RILEY

rather walked into a crime scene of a triple homicide than to be standing here right now. And wasn't that the screwed up part, because I would rather be called to a tragic crime scene to see the horror that waited me inside that house, than to be safe here in a doctor's office.

"Detective Wright, it's good to see you," Alexis said, a warm smile turning up the corners pf her mouth.

Alexis had been Dr. Howard's receptionist for close to ten years now. She was another one of the sweet older ladies that made up the heart of this town. She was always up for a fundraiser and to help organize any event, even at a moment's notice. She believed very strongly that a lady should never show her age, so her hair was always dyed brown to cover any of the

## JADED

grey. She never left her house without wearing makeup and dressed ready to impress. She could be a bit nosy, but if you needed someone to command and corral hundreds of volunteers, Alexis was your girl.

"It's good to see you, Alexis. You look beautiful, as always," I said, flashing her a warm smile. Regardless of how I felt about being here, she didn't deserve for me to take it out on her.

"You are still sweet as honey. You go on back, Dr. Howard is expecting you."

I offered her another small warm smile and then I headed down the hall toward Dr. Howard's office.

I felt like I was a dead man walking to my execution.

It was just an office. There was no threat on the other side of the door.

## EVIE RILEY

There was no man with a gun or a bomb standing on the other side lying in wait. It was just a room with a man sitting in it. There was no danger, and yet, my heart rate was spiking the closer I got to the door. I knew I didn't have a choice, though. I had to go through the door. If I ever wanted to get back to work, I had to do this. I *would* do this because my job was all I had and I was not about to lose it.

Not for anything.

Walking through the door did nothing to slow my pounding heart, but I didn't let it show on me. I closed the door and gave Dr. Howard a simple nod of acknowledgement as I made my way over to the couch that sat across from his chair.

"Detective, it's good to see you," he

# JADED

started.

"Can't really say the same here, Doc," I responded honestly.

I didn't intend to keep it a secret that I didn't want to be here, nor did I feel like I needed to be. There was no point in lying about it. That would only cause problems later on when he quickly discovered I was faking my enthusiasm.

"I get that a lot. I know this wasn't your idea and that you are not all that happy to be here. I take no offense to any of that. Let me start by saying that anything that is said within this room, stays in this room. I'm not going to be mentioning it to anyone outside in the community."

"And I appreciate that, but anyone that sees me walking into this building knows what I'm doing here. People will already talk and whisper about what's going on."

"I don't know much about you, but I do know that you came from New York City and before that I know you did a stint in the army. Most soldiers and law enforcement officers all share the belief that talking to a therapist is a sign of weakness. That you are to hit the erase button within your brain and override all of the horrific images that are stored within your memory box. However, as I am sure you've noticed, there's only so many times the mind can be overridden before all of those horrors explode out and drag you down into the darkness. Sometimes, there are experiences in life that you can overcome without talking about them. Then, there are traumatic horrors that need to be talked about in

# JADED

order for you to ever have a healthy life. I'm not here to judge, Roland. I'm here to listen and to help."

His calm and understanding voice did nothing to ease my racing heart or my nerves. I knew what he said was true. Logically, there was nothing for me to feel ashamed of. That didn't make this any easier, not even the slightest. Letting out a slow and deep breath, I decided to suck this up and get it over and done with.

"I punched Baxter and now Captain Perry believes I need to talk to someone."

"Assaulting another officer is not exactly how things normally work. Have you ever assaulted a colleague before in your career?"

"A few times, yeah. Not like Baxter, it was at crime scenes when there was a

# EVIE RILEY

young gunshot victim and the ambulance was too far away. It went against protocol to transport a victim in a squad car, but if we had waited they would have died. My partner at the time was in agreement with me in taking them in our car, other officers felt differently. I've punched six patrol officers who stood in my way and each time my Captain understood and let it go."

"Well, I can understand that. If it's a choice between saving a child's life and doing nothing, I would pick punching an officer each time. What happened with Baxter, then?"

"He deserved it."

"I'm sure there must have been others over the years that have deserved it as well, but you didn't assault them.

# JADED

What happened specifically with Baxter?"

He wasn't going to let this go and there was no point in trying to stall for an answer. Punching Baxter was the least of my issues and it was the safest topic to be discussing.

"There is a friend of mine who I met three years ago at St. Mark's. Devon. He was homeless, had been since he was seventeen and ran away from his very abusive father. He was able to fall in love with a great young man, got a job, and was accepted into the police academy. Baxter was talking trash about him, about him being gay and homeless. I got tired of hearing it so I knocked him out."

"It must be hard for you being the only gay officer within the police department. I'd imagine when you were

# EVIE RILEY

in New York, you weren't a unicorn over there."

"It wasn't easy in New York, either. Bigger city holds a lot more bigots than the town square could hold. You learn to deal with it and you know who your friends are and which ones just want to watch you burn. I never kept it hidden from day one in the police academy. Moving here, I was honest and straightforward with Captain Perry about being gay and not hiding it. He was fine with it and assured me I wouldn't have to deal with any backwards, redneck comments about it."

"And then Detective Baxter started to make comments about it. But surely that couldn't have been the first time."

"No, he's made jokes and comments for three years now. He doesn't like it,

## JADED

but I have superiority over him and he knows I can knock him out if I wanted to. I normally ignore it."

"But not this time around. Could it be that perhaps there was something else you were dealing with at the time? Another personal issue and you lashed out at Detective Baxter?"

Well, there goes that safe topic. Of course he would try and dig deeper and find some deep root psychological reasoning behind me punching Baxter because I was sick of hearing his bullshit. The trick was going to be getting through three months, two hours a week, sitting here and not divulging any personal or previous issues in my life. It was bound to come up at some point and there was nothing I could do about it. Might as well rip the band-aid

## EVIE RILEY

off and get it over and done with. Letting out a sigh, I spoke as I leaned forward with my elbows on my knees.

"Okay, I am only going to do this once. I did three tours overseas and killed my first person when I was eighteen. In my life, I have shot and killed a hundred and eighteen people, the majority of them men, and all of them were either firing upon me and my team or they had a suicide vest on. Their deaths don't haunt me, because they were trying to kill innocent people. I didn't tell anyone within my unit that I was gay. I kept it hidden, including my boyfriend at the time, Shane, who I loved, lived with, and wanted to marry. He wanted more. He didn't want to be a dirty secret. We got into a huge fight eleven years ago. He stormed out and

## JADED

was killed by a drunk driver twenty minutes later. After three months of the cops not finding the driver, I decided to join the police force and track the bastard down myself. It took two years, and he had killed a mother and her young child in another DUI. I arrested him and was promoted to detective due to my investigation skills. Sometimes, I get nightmares and don't sleep all that great. A combination of my time overseas, losing the man that I love, and working homicides. But that doesn't stop me from doing my job. I was simply sick and tired of hearing Baxter's shit talking, and now he will think twice before doing it."

I made a point of keeping my voice calm and even. I didn't want it shaking with emotions and letting him know how

## EVIE RILEY

much it hurt for me to even say the words out loud to him. I'm not a stupid man. I know it's not normal for someone to be having nightmares every night practically. I know it's not normal for me to be staying awake as long as possible. To be refusing to date anyone, to have not even touched another man in close to eight years.

After Shane had been murdered, I was a wreck. I couldn't even stomach looking at another man, much less touch one. It took three years and a very drunk night at a local gay bar for me to have sex. I would never forget how I felt that next morning, waking up to some stranger in my bed.

The bed that I shared with Shane.

I was sick all day from it and I felt dirty. I felt like I had cheated on him.

## JADED

Ever since, I've been terrified of touching another man, terrified that I would feel that way again. It was just easier to use my own hand when the itch became too much. But that wasn't something that he would understand.

"You've been through a lot in your life. It's natural that you would have days, have nights, where you struggled harder with all of that trauma. Like I said, Roland, I'm not here to judge you. I'm here to help you. To make those hard days and nights fewer in between. To give you ways to cope with them. Do not mistake this as any judgment or me looking for a reason to tell Captain Perry he needs your badge. He doesn't get any reports from me. All I do is sign the form that states you appeared for our session. I'm here to help you work through the

## EVIE RILEY

trauma so you can be healthier. So you can go out and be an even better cop to the people of this town. That's all."

He obviously took what I said as me being defensive, and I probably was.

How could I not be when I was sitting in this position?

"I don't do shrinks," I simply said.

"Most people don't. Don't think of me that way. I've known you for four years. We've worked cases together before, shared beers. I'm not the enemy, Roland, I'm your friend. I'm the one person in this world that you can talk to without any judgments or lectures. If you want to do that in this office, okay, or we can do it in the park with coffee, at a bar after shift. I don't care where we do our sessions, as long as we are doing them. Just not the gym. Please, not the gym.

## JADED

It's extremely depressing how little weight I can lift."

I couldn't help the small chuckle that escaped me. He wasn't old, only thirty-five, but he looked like a wet paper bag could take him out in a fight with a strong gust of wind. He had a wonderful grandmother that was still alive and kicking that could cook comfort food better than anyone I know. Dr. Howard, though, was blessed with a fast metabolism, the only thing he claimed was saving him from obesity. He would have to bulk up quite a bit to even be able to be considered a lightweight fighter, something he made very clear he had zero interest in. He was right. We were friends. He was one of the first friends I made when I moved here. There had been plenty of nights we shared a beer. Plenty of times, when I had unexpectedly unleashed a rant about one case or person to him. I couldn't let the situation around me being here change the fact that we were friends. I wasn't sitting here talking to a therapist. I was sitting here talking to a buddy that just happened to have schooling on how the human mind works.

"Okay, I'll try."

And I would.

He was right. I didn't want to fully admit it right this very second, but he was right.

If I could have fewer horrible days, then why not fight for that?

Men died so I could come home, so I could make something of myself. If I could honor their sacrifice by being a better man, a better cop, and saving

## JADED

more lives, then that is what I needed to do.

Even if that meant facing the darkness within my mind.

# CHAPTER EIGHT

Tyler

THIS WAS SURREAL, absolutely surreal. When Roland had told me he could get me an interview with his buddy, Oswald, I didn't truly believe it would happen. Whether he needed a bartender or not, most business owners didn't hire homeless guys. Yet, last night, when I went to St. Mark's, Roland told me to

## EVIE RILEY

meet Oswald at his bar, Brotherhood Tavern, for an eleven o'clock interview.

Even hearing that I had the chance at a real job wasn't enough to convince me that I truly had a shot. I figured he was just agreeing because Roland was his friend and a cop.

Turned out, I was wrong.

Oswald had already decided to hire me, before I even came through the door. We sat and talked for a good hour about the systems and he told me about his life and I shared some of mine. He didn't care that I didn't have a set address. He didn't treat me like I was worthless or less than anyone. He treated me like every other human being and it almost brought tears to my eyes.

I had been at the bar ever since. I had been working with Tammy, a server, and

## JADED

learning from Oswald how the computer system worked. There was food here and we had a day and night cook. Oswald had explained to me that we were all a team, so if one person needed help, someone would jump in.

For me, I would be the only bartender working at night and on weekends, but Tammy and the other three servers could make drinks as well, if I got slammed. And apparently, I would be getting slammed, especially Thursday, Friday, and Saturday nights. I was just fine with that. I had no problem being busy and working hard. In fact, I preferred it to be busy and having something to do over it being dead and getting paid to stand around.

Tonight was Wednesday and it had been fairly slow all day. I had been training and learning what I could. Tonight, I was going to be closing with Oswald showing me how it all worked, then tomorrow night I was on my own.

I couldn't believe he trusted me this easily. Yes, there were cameras all over the bar, but still, I could easily steal all of his cash and leave town. He would never know until the morning and by then, I would be long gone. I would never do that, but he didn't know that. It was a huge show of trust. One I was not looking to break in any way.

At the sound of the door, I turned to see who was walking in. I was making an effort to know the regulars and remember their drink orders. Tammy said that a lot of the regulars would come around the same time either everyday or every other day after their

## JADED

shift at work.

At the sight of the man that walked through the door, my heart fluttered and that weird feeling was back. I didn't know what it was about Roland, but every time I was around him, I felt so weird. At first, I thought maybe it was my old instinct of fear at his size, but after the diner, I knew that wasn't it. I didn't know what it was, but it had nothing to do with fear.

That feeling completely disappeared at the sight of Jasper walking in right behind him. They were partners, so it only made sense that they would go out for a drink together, but that didn't make it any easier to see him. I instantly wanted to go and hide, but I couldn't. This was my job. I had to speak with him to take his order.

# EVIE RILEY

I could do this.

I *had* to do this.

"Hey, you look good back there," Roland said, flashing me a warm smile.

"Thanks, what can I get for you, Detectives?" I kept my voice even and professional. I wasn't going to let Jasper know his presence affected me.

"Two bottles of Bud, please," Roland answered for them.

I gave a nod and headed over to the beer cooler. I grabbed them each an amber-brown bottle, opening them before bringing them back over.

"Keep the change. This is my partner, Detective Jasper Monroe." Roland handed me the cash for them as he spoke.

"It's nice to meet you, sir."

Jasper grunted and scowled as his

## JADED

only reply.

I could have told Roland that I already knew him, but I wasn't sure if that was something that Jasper wanted him to know. I was sure Roland knew that Jasper was a foster parent, but I didn't want him asking me questions about him and he would if he knew that I was one of his foster kids. It was better to pretend that I had never met him before.

"How is it going? Are you liking it here?" Roland asked next.

"It's good, yeah. Thank you for setting this up. I truly appreciate it."

"Don't worry about it. Oswald is a great guy and he's too old to be working so much. You're doing him a huge favor by taking the job."

Which was exactly what Oswald had

## EVIE RILEY

said. He'd been working a lot without having a night bartender and as energetic as he was, he was older and it wasn't good for him to be working eighty-hour weeks.

I offered them a small smile before I moved on to help the other customers.

Once we were closed, Oswald was going to show me all of the paperwork that needed to be done each night at closing. I was worried about it, especially with how my mind worked, but hopefully it wouldn't be terrible. He was going to walk me through it, though, so with any luck, I would be able to easily follow along with him. It wasn't something I needed to worry about right now. Later, I was sure to be a ball of nerves with it all.

# CHAPTER NINE

Tyler

THE PAPERWORK WASN'T so bad, but I was worried about trying to do it on my own last night. I was not about to tell my new boss that I had some type of learning disability. I would be taking that to my grave. I didn't want to give him a reason to question my abilities or his decision to give me a chance.

## EVIE RILEY

"That's it, Tyler. You did good today," Oswald said, flashing me a warm smile.

Hearing that, it made me feel good. I took pride in my work, no matter what it was. I always strived to do my best and to make my boss happy. It felt good hearing that he was happy with my work.

"Thank you. I truly appreciate you giving me this opportunity."

"Believe me, you are doing me a huge favor. I couldn't find a bartender no matter what I did. You're helping me out immensely with this, Kid. I'll be here tomorrow when you get in, but then I'll be heading home around six. You go on and get out of here. I got some paperwork to finish up and then I'll be right behind you."

"Have a good night, Boss," I said

## JADED

warmly.

"Good night, Kid."

I let myself out the heavy wooden front door and made my way into the back parking lot where my car currently was. I wasn't too sure where I was going to park it moving forward.

Today, I had driven to work because it was a bit of a walk for me in the heat. My asthma was acting up and I tried to avoid having to take my inhaler so it would last longer.

For tonight, I was going to sleep in the parking lot and then tomorrow, before work, I would find a place close by that I could keep my car and sleep in it. It was going to take me a few months to save up enough money for an apartment, even a cheap one, but I would at least be able to start saving up

# EVIE RILEY

money.

Climbing into the backseat, I grabbed the small blanket, quickly set the alarm on my watch, and lay down. I closed my eyes and tried to calm my mind down enough for me to fall asleep.

Some time later, how long I wasn't too sure, there was a knock at my window. Snapping my eyes open, I was fully prepared to see a light from a police flashlight, but instead I was greeted by Oswald's face.

Sitting up, I moved and opened the door, climbing out so we could chat. I wasn't sure what he wanted, but I hoped it wasn't to tell me I was fired.

"Are you sleeping in your car?" he immediately asked me.

"I thought Roland told you I was homeless."

## JADED

I prayed that Roland had disclosed that. I figured he would have and that Oswald had hired me knowing I was homeless. If he didn't tell him, there was no way I would be able to keep this job.

"He told me you were having a hard time finding steady work. He knows I don't care if someone is homeless. I care about them being able to and willing to work."

"I'm not fired?" I asked, holding my breath for his answer.

"God, no. You were great tonight, why would I fire you over being down on your luck? Come on, this way," he said as he waved two fingers at me and headed off to a set of metal stairs attached to the back of the building.

I closed my car door, locked it up, and trotted after him. I had no idea why

## EVIE RILEY

we were going over there, but I was not about to not follow if my boss told me to. I was lucky enough that he wasn't going to fire me over being homeless. I wasn't about to insult him by not following after him.

We trudged up the surprisingly sturdy stairs and he pulled out a key to open the door on the second floor. We walked in, and Oswald flicked on the lights as he cleared the doorway.

I looked around in awe. The place was a small studio apartment with a little kitchenette and a bathroom off to the right. There was a bed off to the right of the kitchenette in the corner and the other half of the room held a small bistro table, loveseat, and a coffee table. It was clean with everything one would need for an apartment in it.

## JADED

"Now, it's not much, I know, but it's got more room than that car of yours."

"What?" Now I was even more confused.

Why was he showing me this?

"I've been sleeping here sometimes at night since I've been having to work the night shift. I use this space as a safe place for my employees. You are not the first homeless person I have hired. Jose, he used to live here up until eight months ago when he was able to secure his own place. I will not tolerate you sleeping in your car. You can stay here, make this your home. You don't pay rent, all you have to do is save up and when you are able to get your own place, you move out and this becomes available to whoever may need it next."

"Boss, I can't stay here for free. You

have to let me pay you something." This was unbelievable. This wasn't actually happening. Tears clouded my vision and my voice wavered slightly at this man's generosity. To say I was overwhelmed would be the least of my emotions at the moment. This sweet, old man couldn't actually not only be giving me a job, but a place to live as well. It was too much. I couldn't possibly accept this.

"You will do no such thing. This place here is for people who need it. I've been doing this for twenty years, now, and have never regretted it for a single second. This is your home, now. Here is a spare key," he said as he held out a key out to me.

Out of instinct, I opened my hand and took it, but I was still in a state of shock. He placed the key in my hand

# JADED

and then placed a comforting hand on my back.

"You'll process this soon enough, Kid. You get some sleep and I will see you tomorrow. Make sure you come down and get some breakfast. I don't want you not eating. You look like a good fart could knock you right over."

I chuckled at that. He was a very straightforward and interesting man. "Thank you for everything. I truly appreciate this."

"We all have hard times in life, it's important to help those that need it. See you tomorrow, Kid."

"Drive safe, Boss."

He waved me off and I could tell he was not a man that liked someone worrying about him. I didn't know much about him at all, really. He had a

## EVIE RILEY

wedding ring on his left hand, so I figured he at least had a wife. He didn't talk about anything personal, though, so as far as kids went, I had no idea. He was well into his sixties and if he had only owned the bar for twenty years, I couldn't help but wonder what he did before that. He didn't seem like a small town guy, so I suspected he moved here, possibly for work. I would have to ask Roland more about him when I saw him next.

Moving further into the apartment, I took a moment to soak it all in. I had an actual roof over my head. I had a small stove and fridge. I could cook food for the first time in four years.

I had a bed.

A *real* bed.

It wasn't some thin old and dirty

## JADED

mattress on the floor. It was a double bed on a bed frame with pillows and a blanket and there were sheets on the bed. I couldn't even remember ever sleeping with sheets on a bed before. It might seem like a small thing to some, but to me it was huge. This was set up as a home, a real home, and I got to stay here.

I stood on the floor of my first real home.

A few tears leaked from my eyes and I didn't bother with wiping them away. I was not going to risk losing my job, losing this opportunity. I was going to show Oswald that I was worth the risk and I was worth all of his generous help.

Sitting down on the loveseat, I sucked in a deep breath to try and calm my emotions down. I would be going to bed

## EVIE RILEY

soon, but first I wanted to take this all in. I never wanted to forget this moment and the joy that it brought to me.

I had never felt actual true joy like I did right now and I wanted to savor this moment for the rest of my life.

# CHAPTER TEN

Roland

THE TRILL OF my phone echoed in the quiet of the night as I sat in my living room. It was just after midnight and old instincts told me there was a crime scene waiting for me. Only, I wasn't in New York City anymore, so the likelihood that my Captain would be on the other end was extremely low. Even though it

# EVIE RILEY

was late, I still picked it up and saw that it was actually Mason, my kid brother.

"You know it's late right?" I said as I answered.

"You know you don't sleep right?" he countered with a light tone.

He wasn't wrong, but apparently he didn't sleep anymore than I did if he was still awake.

"Said the man calling me after midnight. What's going on, little brother, you have a bad dream?"

I was teasing him, but he also knew he could call me even if he did have a nightmare. I would always be there for him. We had no parents, no other family alive, it was just us. He was eighteen when they died, so I didn't have to raise him, but that didn't change that I felt responsible for him.

## JADED

He was twenty-five, now, and worked with Homeland Security going after organizations that committed crimes against children. He traveled all over the country and even overseas when he needed to.

When he told me when he was sixteen that he wanted to be a Federal Agent, my heart went to my throat. I couldn't fault him for it and it wasn't my place to tell him no. By then, I had already been in the Army and was a New York Police Officer. I wasn't in any position to tell him not to do it.

So, I did what I could and made sure he worked out, got fit, taught him how to shoot and how to fight. I couldn't change his mind, but I could make sure he would survive anything that came his way.

## EVIE RILEY

"Just in the middle of a case. These cases, man, they are getting harder and harder. It seems like every time we kill one snake another five show up."

I could hear how stressed and burnt out he was getting. I couldn't do what he did. I couldn't dedicate every waking moment of my life to seeing abused children. He was solving vicious crimes against children and I couldn't be more proud of him.

"You need a break. Come down for a bit and give your mind a rest."

"I've been thinking about that, but I gotta wrap this case up first and it could be a month or more before that happens. I got a shit load of vacation time saved up, so I was thinking about coming down, seeing my big bro, and resetting my brain."

# JADED

"You're welcome here anytime, you know that. You got a room with your name on it, always. You've been doing this for about seven years now, Mason. You need a break before it breaks you."

"I know. I will. What are you doing up still? Or is it one of *those* nights?"

"No, it's not one of *those* nights. Do you remember the kid I was telling you about?"

I had mentioned Tyler to Mason a couple of times over the past few months, about him being young and homeless, and how I hoped to get close enough to earn some trust with him to get him off the street. Mason had advised me to be careful and to reach out to someone within Social Services here, which is what led me to talk to Isaiah.

## EVIE RILEY

"Yeah. Tyler, right? You were looking to see about getting him set up in a foster home."

"Well, it turns out he's not a minor, he's twenty-two and the definition of a baby face. I introduced him to Oswald and he had his first shift as the night bartender tonight."

"No shit? Wow. Well, that's good that he's not a minor, but it's unfortunate that he's homeless and there's nothing you can do about it, really. It's good that he's working, but I don't really understand. Why is that keeping you up?"

"I went there to show my support and I brought Jasper with me. I introduced them and everything seemed fine, but after a couple of beers Jasper told me he actually knew Tyler. That he had been a

## JADED

foster kid with him for two years, between twelve and fourteen."

"Ouch. And Tyler didn't act as if he knew him?" Mason asked, his tone making it clear he was confused as well.

It seemed like a simple thing that could be looked over, but at the same time it didn't sit well with me.

Why would Tyler pretend to not know Jasper?

Why did Jasper never say anything?

He knew I was looking into Tyler's background when I thought he was underage. I had even shown him a photo that I had managed to sneak one night. There was no mistaking his face.

So why didn't he say something then?

"Nope. And I've talked about Tyler before to Jasper, plenty. Even showed him a picture. I'm telling you, there is no

## EVIE RILEY

way you'd forget his face. Yet, Jasper waited until we'd had a few beers last night to tell me. I don't know, it's just not sitting right with me, that's all."

"I agree, I think something is there. It's one thing to not remember a foster kid if they are young, but at the age of twelve, most foster parents remember them. Or if nothing else, they recognize them. You're in a small town, it's not like Tyler was one of thousands that came through his door. You haven't asked Tyler about it yet?"

"No. He works again tonight. I was going to mention it then. We haven't really talked about his time in the system. He was a foster baby, so it's the only life he's known. At the diner the other day, though, he had mentioned that he used to cook for the younger

# JADED

kids and that a dozen eggs and a bag of potatoes could feed six kids for a couple of days."

"That's not enough food," Mason instantly said, before the words could even come out of my mouth.

"That's what I said, but he didn't get into it. I don't know, maybe because it's a small town, I guess I expected foster parents here to be different, but maybe they're not. It's something I'm going to look into, either way."

"Some of the worst foster homes I've come across are the ones in the small danky towns. I'd look into it on my end, too. The least I can do is help you make sure the kids in that town are safe. Let me know if you need any help running any names."

"I will. I'll talk with Tyler tonight and

## EVIE RILEY

see what I can get out of him. I'll loop in Isaiah, too. Doing a check on the current foster homes wouldn't be a bad idea. I'll have to see when the last spot check was done. This is my town. It's bad enough that I can't do anything about the homeless problem we have, I'll be damned if I'm going to turn a blind eye to any problems with children."

"Damn right, Brother. I'll be here if you need me."

"Appreciate it. Now, get your ass into bed, I'll do the same. I love you."

"Love you, too."

I ended the call and stood up to head into the bedroom. I wasn't really tired, but it would be better for me to be lying down at least. Give my body some form of rest and I just might luck out and fall asleep in the process. Tomorrow, or

## JADED

rather tonight, I would talk with Tyler and see what I could squeeze out of him. Hopefully, there was nothing there and it was all just in my head.

# CHAPTER ELEVEN

Roland

THE BAR WAS already busy by the time I got there just after nine. Thursdays were always a good night, and it would leave Tyler with a good amount of tips.

I went and sat on a swivel stool at the bar and watched as he moved around getting drinks for customers and for Tammy. He was a natural behind the

## EVIE RILEY

bar and I loved the confidence he had, even though it was only his second shift. He had made a point of knowing where everything was and how it all worked. He was a hard worker and I knew Oswald would be happy with him. It was a good five minutes before he made his way down toward me and I flashed him a warm smile.

"You're a natural back there."

"Thanks. You want a Bud?"

"Yes, please."

He gave a nod and grabbed an amber bottle from the beer fridge, turning back to slide it across to me.

"Hey, real quick, I know you're busy. I wanted to ask you about Jasper. He told me last night that he was one of your foster parents."

The easy smile on his face slowly

## JADED

disappeared at the mention of Jasper and I kicked myself for being the one who made that smile disappear. It was also concerning, though, and did nothing for my suspicions.

"Yeah, I've had a lot of them. I tend to rather just forget about them and focus on the new set of parents and their rules. I didn't know if people knew he was a foster parent, so I figured I would leave the ball in his court," he said, before he headed off to deal with the customers.

What he said was logical and made sense, yet I couldn't shake the feeling that there was more to this than what he let on. I was still going to be looking into the foster system here in town. I wanted to make sure everyone was safe and okay.

# EVIE RILEY

I spoke to a few people that were around me, but I kept my gaze on Tyler. He was looking good, rested. Oswald had texted me this morning letting me know that he was sleeping up in the studio. He would be getting proper sleep and he would be able to eat properly and hopefully gain some weight. It was a good thirty minutes before he came back my way with another beer.

"Sorry, I've been neglecting you," he offered with a small smile.

"No apologies needed. Everything okay with you? You getting along with the girls and Jose?"

"Yeah, they are great. I um... I actually have a date with Tammy," he said, sounding slightly surprised.

"Really? How did that happen?"

"I honestly have no idea. We were

## JADED

talking and she was mentioning Noelle, her daughter, and next thing I know she asked me out and I said yes. I'm not really sure how it happened," he said with a small shrug and a fake smile.

"Either you have very good game or terrible game." I forced a chuckle out.

"Terrible, it's terrible. I don't know, guess we'll see what happens." He shrugged again before he headed off to grab some drinks for the tables.

I took a long drink from my beer as I tried not think about the fact that he would be going on a date. I had been attracted to him for a while now, I knew that. It got worse once I discovered he was actually legal. At one point, I thought maybe he was into me with the amount of times he'd looked at me or shied away from me, but now I knew for

## EVIE RILEY

a fact that he was into women. The fact hurt more than it should have and it made me slightly sad to know it. I was happy that he was getting his life back on track and going out and meeting people, but it did hurt to know that anything that happened between us would only be in my own fantasies.

# CHAPTER TWELVE

Roland

IT WAS JUST after two thirty when the last customer had finally left the bar. I knew Thursdays were busy nights due to the construction and factory workers that came down on their night off from the nearby towns, but tonight had seemed extra busy for some reason. Oswald had built one hell of a following

## EVIE RILEY

and often the blue-collar workers from the area would make the drive down to have some cold beer and good food. Guess the word about the bar was getting around more these days.

I went over and locked the door while Tyler was looking over some paperwork. He seemed to be lost in his own world as he looked at the checklist that Oswald had behind the bar.

Every night Oswald made sure the inventory was done and the money was counted. He recorded the sales manually, all so he could compare it with the information from the computer. It wasn't that he didn't trust people, it was more that he didn't trust the computer. There had been a few occasions where the computer stopped working and recording part way through

# JADED

the shift, losing valuable information. I had to stop him from smashing it with a hammer on a few occasions.

"You survived. How do you feel?" I asked, flashing him a warm smile as I went over to him.

"It was good. I like being busy," he answered, but I could tell he was a bit distracted as he looked over the paperwork.

I couldn't help but notice the frown that was growing on his face. He was also hovering over the same bullet point for the past couple of minutes. He rubbed his eyes and I couldn't help but wonder if maybe he needed glasses. Perhaps that was why he was having a hard time with the paperwork.

"Everything okay?" I asked gently. I didn't want to insult him or insinuate that he couldn't understand the paperwork.

He let out a tired and frustrated sigh as he looked up at me and I could see the pain and shame in his eyes. I hated seeing it. His eyes were beautiful and they should never be filled with shame or pain, ever.

"When I was in school, the teachers discovered that I had a learning disability, but they didn't know what it was. None of my foster parents wanted to shovel out the money for me to get tested. I have a hard time with reading. The words get all mixed up."

Nodding, I moved around the bar to join him behind it. I spoke as I grabbed two pieces of paper. "My kid brother, Mason, he used to struggle with reading. Finally, when he was twelve, my parents

# JADED

got him tested and it came back that he was dyslexic. The words and letters would jumble together on the page and he couldn't understand any of it. It got worse if he was tired. He still struggles at times, even now, if his mind needs a break. There's a trick we learned, though."

I covered the words on the page with the exception of the very first word. "You have to train your mind to read one word at a time without thinking about it. Once you can do that, then you go to two words, and then three, etc., etc., until eventually, you can read a whole page without any problems. I don't know if you are dyslexic, but the same rule applies."

He straightened up and I could see the determination in his face as he

## EVIE RILEY

started to read a single word at a time. I stood by him, being there to help him if he got stuck on some of the larger words. I knew from Mason that even as a single word, if there were too many letters it could be hard for his mind to read it.

Together, we worked through it all and he was able to write without a problem, something that was a good sign. Mason would often get letters or numbers backward, so at least Tyler didn't have that issue.

He put the paperwork away where Oswald kept it before he came back over and leaned his left hip against the bar top, facing me.

"Thank you for your help and for not making fun of me over it."

"I would never make fun of you over

# JADED

something like this, over anything, but especially something like this. You don't have anything to feel ashamed of, either, Ty. The system failed you, not the other way around. If you want, we can work together on it. I'm not an expert, but I have experience with Mason. I'd be happy to help."

"I would love the help. It's time I started to figure out how to overcome it. It's my life, it's time I took control over it."

"You're off to a great start. I'm proud of you," I said, flashing him a warm smile.

The smile that I got in return, though... Hell, it warmed my whole body. It was the first true smile I had seen on his face, it even reached his eyes. He was the most beautiful man I had ever seen.

## EVIE RILEY

A thought that didn't cause pain to shoot through my heart like it normally did when I looked at another man since Shane.

I don't know what it was about Tyler, but it was as if there was a string connecting us, bringing us together. My hand itched to reach out and touch him. To feel how soft his skin would be underneath my fingers. I had to force myself to remember that he was straight. He was going out on a date with Tammy. There could only be friendship between us.

"It's late, I should get going," I said as I stepped back. I had to get my head back on straight. He was into women, not men.

"Yeah, of course. I'll see you around."

He almost sounded disappointed, but

## JADED

I quickly dismissed the thought. I needed to get out of here and get some space between us. I was not about to jeopardize our new friendship over anything, even if my body wanted his.

# CHAPTER THIRTEEN

Tyler

STANDING OUTSIDE OF Roland's house suddenly seemed like a bad idea.

It had been almost two months since the last time I had spoken with him, truly spoken with him. He had stopped coming by the bar. He was still going to St. Mark's, but I wasn't so we didn't see each other there.

## EVIE RILEY

At the beginning, we'd started meeting for coffee and hanging out, talking with each other during my off hours. I was finally more comfortable around him. Well, at least his size didn't intimidate me so much, anyway. We had been building a friendship. At least, I thought we were.

Then, all of a sudden, he wasn't answering my calls or texts. He'd stopped coming by the bar, and we were no longer meeting for coffee. It was like a light switch had been flipped on our friendship and I had no idea why.

The past two months had been different for me. I had dated Tammy, but that only lasted two weeks before we discovered we were more compatible as friends. I started dating a patron at the bar. Casey. She was a sweet girl and we

## JADED

were the same age. We had a lot in common, outside of me being a foster child. She was a great girl and a lot of fun to be around. It was different to have people in my life all of a sudden.

Friends.

What I couldn't figure out was why Roland was ghosting me all of a sudden and I was done waiting around for him to come to me.

That determination was what brought me to his house tonight on one of my days off. Though, at the time it seemed like a great idea, now, standing here in front of his door, it seemed like the dumbest idea I'd ever had. I could turn back, but I was already here, and if I left, I might never get the courage to come back here and then I would never know what happened.

## EVIE RILEY

I had been going over every conversation we'd had to see if I could have said or done something to offend him or given him any indication that I didn't want a friendship with him. I was coming up blank, though. Something was off. It had to be. Roland was the only one with those answers and I deserved them.

With newfound courage, I reached out and pushed the doorbell before I could change my mind. After a moment, the door opened to reveal Roland, who seemed surprised at my being there. I didn't even wait for him to invite me in. Instead, I started to speak as I walked right through his doorway.

"What is your problem?"

"Excuse me?" he asked, confused, but there was no edge to it.

## JADED

"You've been ghosting me for almost two months now. I deserve to know why you have decided that we aren't friends anymore. What, now that I'm not some pathetic homeless guy on the street you want nothing to do with me?"

That was an actual worry of mine. It might sound illogical, but it was the only logical explanation I could come to that would explain the one-eighty from him. I wasn't about to quit my job and be homeless just so we could be friends, but I deserved the truth, even if it hurt.

"I haven't been ghosting you, Tyler," he denied, but I was not about to let him get away with it. I was not going to tolerate lying.

"Bullshit, Ro. You no longer answer any of my calls or texts. You no longer go for coffee or grab something to eat.

## EVIE RILEY

You're not even coming by the bar anymore. If you have a problem with me, then fine, but say it. And you don't get to take it out on Oswald, he doesn't deserve it after everything he has done..."

My rant was cut short by a pair of lips capturing mine. I hadn't even seen it coming. I was looking just off to the side of him, not directly in his eyes because I still had a hard time with confrontation and it was easier to not look at the person while doing it. His hands were on the side of my face, cupping my cheeks and holding me against his lips.

*His lips.*

Holy shit, I was being kissed by a guy.

Shock didn't seem to cover what I felt in that moment and before my brain could even register what to do, he was

## JADED

pulling back from me.

"That's why I haven't been coming around you. Because every time I'm alone with you, all I want to do is kiss you. I haven't wanted to kiss another man since the man that I loved died eleven years ago. And then you came into my life and it took all of my strength and restraint to not push you up against a wall and kiss the hell out of you. Hearing that you were dating a woman, it killed me inside and I couldn't do it. I thought I could, but I can't. I like you, Ty, and not in a friendly way."

Holy shit.

I needed to say something. I knew I needed to say something, but my mind wouldn't work. All I could feel were his lips still against my own. The tingle that it sent right through my body.

## EVIE RILEY

*Oh God.*

A tingle that still lingered.

I had to say something, anything, right now, but no matter how many times I opened my mouth, no words, no sound would come out.

My instinct to run when being exposed to confrontation or uncomfortable feelings went into overdrive and before I even knew what I was doing, I practically ran out of his house. By the time my mind had caught up to what I was doing, I was ten blocks away. Bending over, I tried to catch my breath. Running was not something I did often and it was not advised with my asthma. I could already feel my chest getting tighter, so I pulled out my inhaler and took two puffs.

Slowly, I felt my lungs start to loosen

## JADED

up. I started back to the bar, walking this time. I hadn't brought my car because Roland actually lived only fifteen minutes away from the bar. It was better to walk than to risk my car breaking down on me. I was saving everything I could to be able to afford an apartment and have a little bit of a cushion, just in case. I had been looking at different apartment for rent ads in the newspaper, so I had a rough idea of the amount I needed to save up. I was about halfway there, as long as my car didn't crap out on me.

*Roland kissed me.*

Fuck, I couldn't get over that. I knew he was gay and I didn't care that he was gay. That was never an issue with me. I didn't think he would ever be interested in someone like me, though. He was built, successful, good looking, he had his life cemented.

Me? I was the exact opposite of that. I was homeless all of two months ago. I didn't have family. I was riddled with trauma that made it hard for me to trust people, especially men. I had no high school education. I didn't even have a diploma. That was all before you factored in my health and my size. I was not attractive to men like Roland. I was barely attractive to women.

How could he possibly be attracted to me?

That wasn't even the most confusing part, though.

I think I liked it.

I could still feel his lips against mine and it didn't bother me. I was a twenty-two year old virgin. It sounded

## JADED

farfetched, but I was.

There was no time growing up to date and have sex because I was not in school and I took care of the younger kids in my foster homes. I couldn't go out on a date. And then, I was homeless and it wasn't like I could bring a girl back to my car.

I had been kissed when I was thirteen by a girl in my foster home, but we never went past heavy make out sessions. The first time I had done anything besides kissing with a girl was Tammy. We had made out plenty of times and we felt each other up, but I never had sex with her. Then, there was Casey, who I had been with for about a month, now, and we still hadn't had sex. It wasn't that she didn't want to, I didn't. When she touched me, yes, I got hard, but I wasn't

## EVIE RILEY

filled with this desire or need to be inside of her.

The lack of desire, I thought maybe that was just how I was wired. Maybe it was normal for me to not want to rip her clothes off. Maybe it was normal for me to not feel sparks when we kissed or touched. But now, I don't know.

Now, I couldn't help but wonder if maybe that was why I didn't feel anything. Maybe I was gay. Maybe that was what this weird feeling I got around Roland was. Maybe it wasn't fear, but attraction. I don't know. The more I thought about all of it, the more confused I got. I needed time. Time to think and figure out who I was and what gender I was attracted to.

The second I arrived back at the bar, I got into my car and headed over to

## JADED

Casey's place. I needed to talk to her. I had no idea what I was going to do, but I did know it wasn't fair to her to wait while I figured it all out. If I was actually attracted to men over women, I wasn't about to string her along and I was not about to hide who I was.

That was something I was confident in. Once I knew who I was and I accepted it, I was not going to be hiding in any closets. I just needed to figure out what gender I was attracted to. I needed time to process the events that happened and my own feelings.

Pulling up to Casey's apartment, which was the bottom level of a house, I parked and turned off the engine. I wasn't sure what I was going to tell her, but I wasn't about to lie. I would still see her at work and I didn't want to cause any hostility. Letting out a slow breath, I climbed out of my car and strolled to her door. She opened the door a moment after I knocked and I could see she was pleasantly surprised to see me.

"Baby, what are you doing here?"

"Sorry, I should have called or texted first. There's just something I need to talk to you about. Can I come in?" This was not a conversation I was about to have over the phone and definitely not through text messages. She deserved better than that.

"Of course, yeah," she said as she moved back.

Normally, I would kiss her and I could tell she expected one, but I couldn't bring myself to do it. I was afraid that if my lips touched hers that I would lose the feeling of Roland's lips. I

## JADED

wasn't ready for that yet.

"What's on your mind?" she asked as she closed the door.

I didn't even know where to start. When Tammy and I called it quits, she started the conversation off and I jumped on it. Maybe being honest was the best way to go here.

"A guy just kissed me," I blurted out.

"Wow, are you okay?" she asked sincerely as she walked over to her couch.

"I didn't kiss him back and it came out of nowhere." I spoke as I joined her. The last thing I wanted was for her to think I was cheating on her.

"I know you well enough to tell that you aren't the cheating type. You know, I would be lying if I said I hadn't wondered if you were gay," she said carefully.

## EVIE RILEY

"What?"

"I don't mean it against you at all. I have a few gay friends, both guys and girls. It's the twenty-first century, love who you want. But yeah, I've wondered. A girl can tell when a guy isn't all that hot and heavy into her. I didn't want to push, figured maybe you were trying to work something out yourself."

Of course she would have noticed. I should have figured as much. It would be pretty obvious that I wasn't dying to get in her pants when every time she tried to move things along I put the brakes on it.

"Honestly, I don't know. I've never looked at a guy that way before, but if I'm honest with myself, I've never looked at a girl like that before, either. Dating wasn't a thing for me growing up. There

## JADED

was no time for it. I haven't really put any thought into it."

"When you kiss someone, especially the first time with that person, it leaves you feeling like electricity just shot through you. Your whole body is covered in goosebumps and you tingle. Have you ever felt that way when you kiss a girl?" she asked with complete patience and understanding in her voice. She wasn't mad that we were having this conversation. Apparently, she had been waiting for it.

"No. I'm sorry, that sounds mean considering what we've done." The last thing I wanted to do was make her feel bad.

"It doesn't sound mean at all. Lots of people can have a great time together, a great friendship, but zero chemistry. It happens all the time. The world didn't move when I kissed you either. There's no deep love between us and that's okay. There's nothing wrong with us being friends. What did you feel like when he kissed you, beyond the obvious shock and surprise."

"Shock and surprise mostly sums it up. It happened so fast and it didn't last long, I didn't even have the chance to respond or push him away. Afterward, though, there was that tingling feeling. It wasn't strong, but there was something there."

That was the confusing part, because apparently I should have felt that way kissing her, but I didn't. Maybe I was gay, maybe this was a piece of myself that had been missing, a piece I didn't know was missing. This conversation

## JADED

had me feeling better in the sense that I wasn't hurting her by breaking up. However, it was only leaving me even more confused by how I felt toward Roland.

"I think the best thing you can do is take some time to be single and let your mind process everything that happened. Right now, it's all new and your mind is probably overloaded with new feelings. Take your time and see how you feel about it in a few days. Then try and think about what you want."

She was right. I needed to take some time to myself, process, and then re-evaluate my feelings toward Roland. I'd give myself a week to be on my own, in my own world, and hopefully, by the end of the week, I'd have a better grasp on what I wanted.

# CHAPTER FOURTEEN

Roland

HOW COULD A single week feel like an eternity?

It had only been a week since Tyler stood here in my home with my lips against his. It was a single moment in my life that was both good and horrific.

Horrific, because it caused Tyler to flee from not only my home, but from his job as well. He hadn't been to the bar in the past week and that was all my fault.

It was also good for me, though, because of how amazing it felt to feel his lips. To feel him against me. I never thought I could ever feel that way toward another man, not since Shane. I would have sworn on my life that Shane was my soulmate. That he was who I was meant to be with. Yet, one single sort of kiss with Tyler and the world moved. I had never felt that way with Shane, which brought on its own confusion.

During my session with Dr. Howard, he could tell that something was off with me. I had been a bit depressed, something that got worse as the days without seeing Tyler added up. He had explained that perhaps at the time I believed that Shane was the only guy for

## JADED

me in this life, that he was my soulmate, it was because he was the only male I had been with. He described it as puppy love, often what teenagers feel, versus true love. He mentioned that it is normal for young people to feel this way until they become an adult and they go through a few relationships and eventually discover that what they felt when they were younger was nothing compared to the real thing.

I didn't want to believe that Dr. Howard could be right, but as each day went on, that single kiss invaded my entire body and mind. I dreamed about Tyler and his lips all over me. My lips all over his body. Being inside of him. My thoughts of him were all consuming, all from a single kiss.

Maybe what I did have for Shane was

puppy love. Maybe I clung to him and his memory so hard, because that's who I believed to be my soulmate, like most teenagers.

It hurt to think of Shane like that and I knew he would always live within my heart, but it was possible that he didn't need to live in my whole heart. He could live in a piece of it as my first love. I hoped that maybe, just maybe, over time, the hurt would decrease until I no longer felt it. One thing I did know from kissing Tyler, I could have a chance at finding love again one day.

My problem, though, I craved Tyler and his body. Not just his body in a sexual sense, but his presence. I had grown used to having him around. To grab a coffee or a meal together. To see him at the bar after a long day of work.

## JADED

He had become the best part of my day and now for the past week that sunshine was gone. It had been pouring rain and no matter what I did I couldn't escape it.

I hadn't even been to the gym all week because I didn't feel like doing anything. I would drag my ass to work and to my sessions, but then just come right back home and sit on the couch. Eventually, my eyes would start to burn from exhaustion and then I would crawl into bed just to be haunted by dreams of him. It was exhausting and it dragged me down more than anything ever had before.

A knock at my door brought me out of my depressing spiral. Letting out a tired sigh, I mentally debated if I should get up or not. It couldn't be anyone important, because if it was they would have called me.

The knock came again.

I forced my body to move and get up. Whoever it was on the other side of my door, they were clearly not going away. I wasn't sure who I expected, but when I opened my door the last person I expected stood there.

Just the sight of Tyler was enough for my heart to jump right into my throat. For a week, I had been worried about him. For a week, I had been terrified that I had scared him off and he had left town. That he had thrown all of his progress away because of my reckless actions. Oswald had said he had asked for some time off, but that didn't ease my fears.

"Hey, um... can we talk?" he asked with complete uncertainty to his voice.

## JADED

I hated hearing it. I used to hear it all the time when I first met him. He wouldn't make eye contact with me and he would often shy away, stutter. But we were past that, or so I thought. I hated that I was responsible for putting that timidness back into him.

"Yeah, of course. Come in," I said as I moved back and he cautiously walked into my house.

He was a ball of nerves and I knew I had to be careful with my actions and words toward him. I didn't want to scare him off again. I had no idea how we were ever going to get back to being friends with each other, but I was determined to make it happen. If there was one thing that I had discovered this past week, it was that I didn't want him out of my life. Even if that meant we would only ever be friends. He was special and I was not about to lose him again.

"Look, Ty, I'm sorry. I shouldn't have kissed you. It was wrong of me. It came out of nowhere for me, too. I knew I had been attracted to you, but I never thought I would act on it. I know you're straight," I started, but he cut me off with a very soft and confused voice.

"I don't know about that."

"Don't know about what?"

"I'm confused. I've never looked at guys like that before, but I've never looked at women like that, either. Growing up, I just thought I was too busy to notice and then I was homeless. I didn't have sex with Tammy or Casey. I've never had sex with anyone. The interest or desire to have sex has never been there. I just thought it was *me*. But

# JADED

then, you kissed me and now I can't stop thinking about it. When you kissed me, my whole body tingled from it and the feeling lasted for hours afterward. I've never felt that way before. So, yeah, I'm confused and I just needed some time to process what happened. To try and figure out what I felt."

Two thoughts ran through my mind. The first, *holy shit he's a virgin.* The second, *he might be gay.* I thought the possibility of me and him having some type of a romantic relationship was completely off the table, but now it was actually on the table. There was a true chance that we could build something, if that is what he wanted. It made sense why he needed time.

I could still painfully remember what it was like for me when I first discovered

## EVIE RILEY

I was gay. Mason had handled it so much easier than me. He was fine with it, accepted who he was since he was twelve.

Me, though, I denied it. I tried everything within my power for me to fit within the straight box. I dated a lot of girls. I was a player and I kept having sex with them. I was going to be straight, because I couldn't be the gay soldier. Even at the age of sixteen, I knew I was going to be in the army and I knew I couldn't do that as a gay man.

But no matter how many women I slept with, I never felt satisfied.

On my eighteenth birthday, a week before I was to ship out for boot camp, I went to a gay club with my fake ID. It was there that I met Shane and we hooked up that night. The first time

# JADED

being touched by another man sent fire all down my spine. I could still feel his touch lingering long after we had parted. I knew exactly what Tyler was feeling right now.

"When you've gone your whole life believing and thinking you were straight, it's not easy to accept that you could actually be gay. Taking the time to be alone and to gather your thoughts was the best thing you could do, Ty. There's no pressure here. We can pretend that the kiss never happened and just go back to being friends. You have the control here."

The last thing I wanted was for him to feel pressured into being with me. If he wanted to be with me, I wanted it to be because he felt attracted to me and not out of some sort of obligation. I didn't want anything fake. I wanted something real between us.

"I don't think I want that. To go back to just being friends, I mean. But I've never done this before and I don't know if I'll even be any good, at the sex or the relationship part. But, I want to try. I know when you kissed me I felt electricity for the first time in my life and I know I want to feel that way again. I just need you to be patient with me while I try and figure it all out."

"We have all the time in the world. We'll take it slow and you dictate what you are ready for in terms of the sex department. We'll go as slow as you need. I'm not in any rush."

Sex was an important part in a relationship in terms of chemistry and connection, but it also wasn't the only

## JADED

part. I wanted to connect with Tyler on an emotional and mental level as well and not just a physical one. I had no problem waiting to have sex with him. Hell, it'd been eight years since I'd had sex. He wouldn't be the only one nervous and unsure.

"Will you..." he started, but then stopped, clearly scared and unsure.

I moved closer to him, placed my hand on the side of his face, and tilted his head so he was looking at me and not the ground. He needed to start building up some confidence. He needed to understand and learn that he was not less than in any way. Especially to me.

"Will I what? You can ask me anything, Sweetheart."

I never wanted him to hesitate with me. He needed to feel like he could be open and honest with me. I wanted him to feel like he could tell me anything or ask me anything. I didn't want secrets between us. If we were going to have any chance of a real relationship, we needed to build a strong foundation.

"Will you kiss me?" he asked softly.

"Always." I closed the small distance between us. This time, when I pressed my lips against his, I kept it soft and gentle. Last time, I had kissed him out of raw need, and this time I wanted to savor it. I wanted him to savor it.

His lips were softer than I remembered them being. He felt amazing and unlike last time where he froze at the contact, this time he pressed back. He was still unsure and slightly apprehensive. I could feel it. I understood it.

## JADED

When I first kissed Shane, even though I had been kissing girls for years, I felt like I didn't know how to do anything. I knew, though, that Tyler would get more comfortable and loosen up. Soon, the pleasure would kick in and he would take more control.

He started to get a bit braver as he pressed his lips a bit harder against mine. I moved and his lips easily followed me. I could feel his body starting to loosen up, so I pushed my tongue out to trace against his lips, asking for permission, which he easily gave. The second I felt his tongue against mine, we both moaned. He tasted better than I ever could have imagined.

He ran his hand up along my chest as I moved us back so his back was up against the wall. I wanted nothing more than to press against him fully, but this was only a kiss. I needed to go slow and let him dictate how fast we took things. It wasn't even the fact that being with a guy was a new experience for him. It was the fact that he was a *virgin*.

Your first time is supposed to be special, something I didn't believe in when I was younger, but I did believe in it now. He deserved for his first time to be romantic and sweet, especially after all of this time. I could have kissed him all night, but we needed to talk more first.

Reluctantly, I pulled back, stopping the kiss in its tracks. He gave a small whine at the loss of contact and that was a very good sign. He liked it and wanted more. Hopefully, that would help ease

# JADED

some of his confusion about his new discovery.

"Wow," he said softly.

I let out a warm chuckle. I was feeling the same way.

"Come on, let's sit down and talk."

If we were ever going to have any chance at something real, I needed to be honest with him. And that meant telling him about Shane. It wasn't going to be easy at all, it was going to hurt to talk about, but I knew I had to do it. I had been talking to Dr. Howard about it in between my stories from my army days. It was hard, but I had to admit, it was helping. We went and sat down on my couch and I turned so I could face him.

"You shared something very personal with me and it's only fair that I do the same. First, I want to let you know, though, that I would like to build something real with you. It's not about sex, and like I said, we will take it as slow as you need. There's no pressure on my end."

"I'd like to build something with you, too. I'm not good at this and I don't really know how to be in a healthy relationship, but I'm willing to learn."

"To be honest, I don't really know, either. I've only dated one guy in my life. *Shane*. He was the first guy I had kissed when I turned eighteen. I didn't handle it well when I discovered I liked boys over girls. I still tried to like girls, to fit into the box I thought I had to be in. I slept with thirty girls between sixteen and eighteen, but none of them ever left me feeling satisfied. Friction was the only reason I could even get off. But a week

## JADED

before I was to leave for boot camp, I decided to go to a gay club. It was there I met Shane. We were together for three years, but I kept him a secret. I stayed in the closet and it was a serious issue for Shane. He was out and proud and he didn't like being a dirty secret. We got into a huge fight when I was twenty-one and he stormed out and drove off. He was hit by a drunk driver. He was dead on impact."

"I'm so sorry. I can't even imagine."

"It was hard. It was *really* hard. I was set to go into the Rangers, but his death changed everything. They didn't find the driver and that wasn't something I could live with. I joined the police force in New York City and, eventually, I was able to find the man that killed Shane. I came out when I went into the academy. I

## EVIE RILEY

wasn't going to make the same mistake twice. It took three years, though, before I could bring myself to touch another man. The next morning, I felt horrible. I felt like I had cheated on Shane. I swore I would never feel that way again, so I haven't been with anyone in eight years. You are the first man that I have kissed in eight years."

I could see the shock flicker across his eyes. It was surprising and that was why I never told anyone. Whenever someone at work asked me about my dating life, I kept it private and said it was none of their business. To go eight years without sex seemed unheard of where a guy was concerned. Even more so when you factor in I hadn't even touched a man in eight years.

"Really?"

## JADED

"Yes. So all of this is new to me again. I wanted you to know that so you can completely understand and believe me when I tell you that sex isn't important to me. We can take as long as you need. If all we do is kiss, I'm good with that. The most important aspect is you feeling comfortable with taking any of the next steps."

"Thank you for sharing that with me." He reached over and placed his hand in mine as he spoke. "As much as you want me to be comfortable, I want the same for you. I don't want you doing anything that you aren't ready for either."

"I promise."

It was an easy promise for me to make. One that I would be keeping, and I knew he would keep his promise as well. Tonight had gone so much better

## EVIE RILEY

than I had ever expected. I never thought I would even get to see Tyler again. Now, here we were sitting on my couch and actually going to start a relationship together. It was a dream come true and I couldn't wait to see what the future held for us.

# CHAPTER FIFTEEN

Tyler

LISTENING TO ROLAND tell me about Shane really cemented my certainty for him. I was a bit worried that he was looking for sex right away, or that he wasn't looking for a relationship. He was older than me by ten years. We were at two different places in our lives and it would be natural that he wasn't looking for anything serious. It felt amazing to know that he wanted to take things slow with me, too. That he wanted to build a strong foundation with trust and honesty on both of our ends so we could form a strong relationship. It matched everything that I knew about him and it only made me feel more certain that I was making the right choice.

It hurt to hear him talk about Shane. Not because I was jealous, but because I could hear the pain still in his voice. Even though it had been eleven years, that wound was still fresh and had yet to scar over. I'm sure some would feel like they were competing with a ghost, but I didn't feel that way. I had never loved someone before, but I could imagine that if I lost the man that I loved, that I thought I would marry and be with

## JADED

forever, it would be devastating. He needed to heal from it and I had no problem helping him heal. I had no problem listening to stories about him. I already knew he must have been a special man if Roland loved him so deeply.

We decided to put on a movie and just relax on the couch together. I had to work tomorrow night and I was looking forward to going back to the bar. When I had asked Oswald for the week off, he was very sweet and kind about it. I was worried he would deny my request, but he was good with it and he didn't push to know why. I'd tell him my reasons tomorrow so he knew I wasn't just taking time off to flake on him or because I didn't feel like working. He had been nice enough to not only give me a job, but a place to live and the last thing I wanted was for him to feel taken advantage of or that I was ungrateful.

I was trying to pay attention to the movie, I really was, but it was a lot harder than I thought it would be. Feeling the heat from Roland's body right next to me, all I could think about was how good it felt to feel his lips on mine. I wondered how his body would feel against mine.

If the weight of him would leave me feeling claustrophobic or safe.

I was still trying to get used to all of this. To being attracted to him, to a man, but also being interested in sexual activities. I was also still trying to get used to him being huge.

My whole life I had been afraid of men that were big, much less massive like he

## JADED

was. I kept reminding myself that he wasn't going to hurt me. That I didn't need to flinch and curl up whenever he got too close to me. That when he reached out for me, it wasn't to grab and hurt me. The fear, the reaction, was deeply ingrained in me and I knew it would take time for that instinct to be erased. But I also knew he had been good about it.

He always made a point of making sure I saw when he moved his hand toward me. Even little touches here and there to help me get used to his presence. The signs were there that he had been developing feelings for me, but to me those little touches weren't affectionate, just a man moving around. Knowing that they were actually affectionate touches, it left a warm

## EVIE RILEY

feeling in my chest.

We were halfway through the movie, but I truly had no idea what was going on with it. I was looking at the screen, but my mind wasn't taking any of it in. I couldn't focus on anything but his body. The feel of his lips against mine. He was allowing me to have complete control over our situation, meaning he wouldn't kiss me again tonight until I initiated it.

The problem was, I didn't really know how to do that.

With a girl it was easy, and more times than not, she would be the one to initiate it with me. Normally, by sitting on my lap and kissing me. I wasn't really sure how to go about initiating it with Roland, but if I wanted to feel his lips against mine again, I would have to figure it out. The only thing I could think

## JADED

of would be to straddle his lap.

I mean, if it works for a girl, why wouldn't it work for me?

Right?

*Oh God.*

Gathering up all of my courage that I could muster, I moved and straddled his lap, snapping his attention away from the movie. He gave me a warm smile as I started to close the gap between our lips.

The second our lips touched, a fire shot right through me. I had never felt this way before and it was all consuming. The need for more, the need to feel his body against mine, it was overwhelming in a good way. This time around as we kissed, I moved my hands up and down his chest, feeling each and every single muscle that was lying underneath his shirt.

## EVIE RILEY

His hands ran down my back and landed on my ass. He squeezed it slightly, causing my hips to rock forward just the slightest, but it was enough for our crotches to rub together. That slight touch was enough to cause me to moan and I needed to feel it again.

I rocked my hips, causing friction between us and, apparently, I wasn't the only one with the desperate need to feel it again, because Roland used his grip on my ass to rock my hips even more. We both moaned and I could feel his dick was already hard, straining against his pants. I was already hard and to feel his dick throbbing against mine, with only material separating us, was pure and utter bliss.

I picked up my pace and Roland started to roll his hips to match mine. It

# JADED

added to the friction and we were both moaning and panting. I had to pull back from the kiss as it became too hard to keep going while we were moving.

"Oh fuck," I moaned.

Never in my life had I ever felt this good before. Not even with my own hand or that from a female.

"That's it, just feel it, Baby," Roland said as he started to kiss and nibble along my neck.

That's all I could do right now, was *feel.*

Everything around us disappeared. I couldn't even hear the movie anymore. All I could hear were our moans and heavy breathing echoing throughout the room. All I could feel were his hands on my ass, his lips on my neck, and his glorious thick dick against my own.

## EVIE RILEY

It was like everything in my life was clicking at this exact moment. Gone was the confusion of being attracted to men. Gone was the uncertainty if this was the right call to make. Our bodies fit together so perfectly, and it felt too good to be anything but real and right. I was gay and I was going to embrace every aspect of it.

I had no idea how the sex aspect would work. I had to assume that it would be my ass that he would be pounding into and not the other way around. It was slightly terrifying, but if he could make this feel good and we weren't even skin to skin, shit, I couldn't wait to see how good it would feel when I could feel every inch of his body and dick against my own.

Our panting and moans picked up

## JADED

and I could feel his dick hardening more against mine. We were both close to the edge and I was torn between wanting to come and wanting to hold off so we could keep doing this. I wasn't ready for the pleasure to end, but my body had other thoughts in mind. After a moment, I was coming hard in my own pants, something I had never done before.

"Ro," I moaned deeply as he continued to move my hips up and back over his cock so he could follow behind me.

I pulsed as I listened to his delicious grunts as his own climax quickly approached. He held my hips down over his dick as he gave a deep groan and then I could feel his dick pulsing underneath me. The feeling of it caused my own dick to pulse in return, pumping me for even more cum.

I placed my forehead against his as we both fought to regulate our breathing. Everything was tingling, absolutely everything, even my lips. I knew it was from a combination of pleasure and lack of air from panting so much.

"That was the best movie I've ever seen," he joked.

I couldn't help but laugh at that. It was a great movie. One that I would be very interested in seeing over and over again.

"Well, that cleared up any confusion. I'm definitely gay."

It was his turn to laugh at that. Not having that confusion hanging over me, over us, was going to be a huge relief. At least I knew for a fact that I was gay,

## JADED

completely, and we could work on building a strong relationship. I would also hopefully not be scared or as nervous with the next aspect of our sexual relationship as we progressed.

"I'm glad we could clear that up for you. Now, we're both sticky and tired. I haven't come in my pants since I was a teenager."

"I've never done it. I have to agree, though, things are getting a bit sticky."

The journey to get here had been amazing, but now that the pleasure was starting to taper down, I was getting a bit uncomfortable with wet cum in my pants. It wasn't a fun and enjoyable feeling, but I knew I would be more than willing to go through it again.

"Come on, let's turn in. I have a spare room you can sleep in. As much as I

## EVIE RILEY

would like to have you in my bed, I don't think either of us would be able to keep our hands to ourselves and I don't want to move too fast."

That might actually be the sweetest thing I had ever heard. He truly did want to take things slow and he was making sure I would be comfortable with whatever we did. It was sweet and I greatly appreciated it.

He was also right.

I don't think I would be able to keep my hands to myself if I was in bed with him. I could have walked back home, but I was exhausted and wanted to get cleaned up. Plus this way, I would get a good morning kiss and that was very appealing to me.

"Sounds good," I easily agreed.

I got up off his lap and he turned off

## JADED

the TV and the lights before we made our way up the stairs. He showed me where the bathroom was and the spare bedroom. He had his own bathroom in his room. He gave me a slow and passionate kiss that left my knees weak and had my dick half hard by the time he pulled back.

"Good night, Sweetheart," he said warmly.

"Good night, Babe."

He gave me a wink before he turned and headed down the hall to his own bedroom to get cleaned up himself.

I watched as he walked away, noticing his ass and how amazing it looked in his jeans before he disappeared. Letting out a soft sigh, I headed into the bathroom to get cleaned up. Tonight had been a whirlwind of

## EVIE RILEY

emotions, but I was glad I had decided to take the risk and come here. It had more than paid off and I couldn't wait until the morning when I could see him again.

# CHAPTER SIXTEEN

Roland

JUST AS THE coffee finished percolating, my front door opened and I heard the telltale sound of clicking against my floors. The smile that rushed over my features was instant as I turned and saw Koda running straight for me as Mason closed the door. Koda was Mason's gorgeous German Shepherd that he

## EVIE RILEY

trained for work. The sight of the dog filled my heart with happiness.

Koda was five years old now, but he was still full of energy. He was the sweetest dog. Mason got him when he was just eight weeks old and started to get him trained. After five years, he was now trained for attack, scent tracking, and to detect anxiety. Mason often used him with the children he came across in his job, and Koda had made a huge difference to thousands of children. Whether they were anxious with being away from the only life they had known, or they were too scared to sleep at night, Koda was there for them and made them feel better, made them feel safe.

I was thankful that my brother had companionship in Koda. I knew the horrors that he often saw with his job,

# JADED

and Koda would be there to protect and help him heal from the toll it could take on him.

"Hello, my sweet boy," I said as I started to pet him. "You know he loves me better, right?" I teased my brother, who very maturely rolled his eyes.

"He only likes you because you slip him food from the table when you think I'm not looking."

I chuckled at that, because I really thought I had gotten away with it. It never failed, though, every time I saw Koda I always told myself that I should get a dog, yet I still haven't. Maybe this time around I would.

"How was the trip?" I asked as I reluctantly moved away from Koda and gave my brother a hug.

Mason was not built like me, but he

## EVIE RILEY

was still muscular and I knew for a fact he could take anyone in a fight. I had trained him, after all. We did look similar, though, in terms of our hair and eye color, the shape of our face. We were both cursed with being handsome and, oddly enough, were both gay.

"Not bad. Airplanes are nothing for me."

No truer words had been spoken. Mason was built for flying. It didn't matter if it was two hours or twenty-four hours, he could do it standing on his head. I was all right with flying, but those long flights were not something I had missed since being out of the army.

"So, what's been going on since I talked to you last? You seem to be in a better mood than you were a few days ago. I expected to find you on the couch

## JADED

in sweatpants with empty pizza boxes and beer cans all around you."

That wasn't all that inaccurate.

I really wish it was, but a few more days and I probably would have reached that level. I wasn't a health freak, but I usually did make sure I ate right. It wasn't often I would eat greasy pizza, but if I did then you could assume I was feeling sad or stressed.

"Tyler came over last night. We had a great conversation."

"Oh, just a conversation?" he teased as he grabbed some coffee and headed for the table.

"A bit more than that. It started off with a conversation. He told me that he needed time to get his feelings in order and to process everything that had just happened."

## EVIE RILEY

"Makes sense. He thought he was straight his whole life. Having a guy kiss you out of nowhere can be shocking.," Mason said with complete understanding in his voice.

"And that was my fault for doing it that way. It came out of nowhere. Thankfully, though, I didn't scare him off for very long. He told me he had feelings for me, too. That he didn't even sleep with the two women he had been dating in the past two months. He's actually never slept with a woman before, or anyone."

"Damn, you bagged yourself a twenty-two year old virgin. Now I'm jealous."

I couldn't help the sigh. My brother, he was a sucker for smaller guys and virgins. They were his kryptonite and I swear one day he was going to sleep with

# JADED

the wrong guy and be on the wrong end of a gun.

"The point is, we are taking things slow. We watched a movie and made out a bit last night before we went to sleep, in separate rooms. I'm trying to make him feel comfortable and allow him to stay in control of the sexual progress."

It wasn't easy, because I would have loved to have him underneath me. However, I did remember what it felt like to first discover you were gay. It was terrifying and confusing. The last thing Tyler needed was for me to be a jerk and pressure him to go faster.

"I am happy for you. It's been a very long time since you've allowed yourself to be with another man. I know what happened with Shane was devastating, but you've kinda been putting your whole life on pause, Bro. I don't know what it's like to lose the man you love, and I didn't know Shane as well as I should have, but he wouldn't want this for you. He wouldn't want you to be alone and heartbroken for the rest of your life."

His voice was calm and gentle and it reminded me of the voice he often used with child victims. What he said was true and I knew that. Shane wouldn't want me to be miserable. The whole point of the fight was he wanted me to come out of the closet. For us to have a true relationship and potentially get married. He wouldn't want me to be alone and miserable forever. It was something I was trying to deal with during my sessions with Dr. Howard.

"I'm trying. What about you? Any new

## JADED

men in your life?"

"Not right now, no. I've been too busy with work. I'm not really the dating type, anyway. It's easier to keep things to friends with benefits or one-night stands."

"Always such a romantic," I teased, sarcasm lacing my voice.

Before he could comment, Koda's head snapped up and looked right at the door. I caught the tension that flared through my brother's body and I couldn't help but wonder if more was going on with him then he had been telling me.

"You expecting someone?" He tried to keep his voice calm and casual, but I could hear the tightness in his voice. He was on edge. Something else was definitely going on with him. I knew he

## EVIE RILEY

wouldn't talk about it right now, but I would be keeping an eye on him.

"It's Isaiah. He's coming by so we can talk about the foster home situation," I answered as I got up to let him in.

I had told Mason about Jasper and Tyler's reaction to him. Even after Tyler tried to blow it off, I still felt uneasy about it, so I reached out to Isaiah to see what he could discover for me. He had called last night before Tyler came over to tell me he found something and we needed to talk about it. He wanted to come over last night, but I knew Mason would be here in the morning and told him to come by now. If something was going on, it helped to have a Federal Agent around.

"Hey man, come on in," I said warmly as I opened the door.

## JADED

Where I looked well rested, a strange thing for me because I didn't have a single nightmare last night, Isaiah looked like a train wreck. His hair stood in spikes around his head and there were dark rings around his eyes. If I didn't know him better, I'd assume he'd gone on a bender and this was the end result. But, I did know him better. This was no bender. I had no idea what he had discovered, but it looked like it had him up all night tossing and turning.

"Is your brother here?" he asked as he walked in.

"Yeah, in the kitchen. Come on back and grab a coffee. You look like you could use it. Rough night?"

"You wouldn't believe what I found, Roland," he said as we headed toward my kitchen.

## EVIE RILEY

I had no idea what he had found, but by how he was behaving, he found something huge. Something I wasn't going to like. I did the introductions as Isaiah grabbed some coffee.

"Mason, this is Isaiah. He works with Social Services and is who I mentioned that I reached out to about intel on Tyler."

"It's nice to meet you," Mason said with a nod as he held his hand out to Isaiah.

"Nice to meet you. I have a feeling we're going to need your help on this one." Isaiah clasped my brother's hand in his easily as he spoke.

"What did you find?" I asked, getting things started.

"I started by looking through Tyler's time with Jasper. As you know, he was

# JADED

there between the ages of twelve and fourteen. He was one of eight foster kids, sometimes a little less, over the two years. It all seems perfectly normal and there weren't any red flags in Tyler's file for Jasper. Before that, he had been through a lot of rough homes and had been abused. It all stopped for two years before he was sent to another foster home and then it picked up all over again."

"Okay, but I'm not hearing anything to imply that something is wrong with Jasper. Sounds like you need to review all of the foster homes in the system, though," Mason said.

"Tyler was diagnosed with a protein deficiency when he was eight. It makes it hard for him to gain weight. Aside from that and the asthma, he was perfectly healthy. Broken bones and bruising, but no illnesses. For the two years he was with Jasper, everything was perfect. *Too perfect.* Bruises were gone, he went to school, everything was normal and without complaint. Then all of a sudden, he's being transferred, at Jasper's request, to another home and the hell started all over again. Only, he was there for two days when he started to get very sick. His social worker saw how sick he was and took him to the hospital. They ran his blood work and discovered he was going through cocaine withdrawal." Isaiah ran a hand through his hair, mussing it even more.

"Whoa, what?"

I wasn't expecting that. I figured maybe Jasper had lost his temper with him at times and hurt him. Jasper did

## JADED

have a temper on him and if you pushed the right button he lost his shit. I had seen it at work before. We had been partners for three years now, but I thought I knew him. I thought I had seen the ugliness he had inside of him.

"There was no way of telling how it got into his system, just that it was there. His social worker asked where he got the drugs, but he clammed up. They brought Jasper in to be questioned, but he was a Detective, even back then, so the worker believed everything he said. He said Tyler must have gotten it from school, that he had no idea. They went with Jasper's story and never looked into his home or any of the other children." Isaiah shook his head.

"It's not uncommon for children in their young teenage years to get their

## EVIE RILEY

hands on cocaine. I find it hard to believe that no one would have noticed. If he was going through physical withdrawal, he'd have had to have been doing it for months and in large doses. Were any of the other children checked out?" Mason asked.

"That's the thing, the social worker never spoke to any of the current children or looked through his home. So, I did." He placed a rather large brown file on my table as he continued.

"That is Jasper's and Dana's fostering file. It includes every child they have ever taken in, including the current ones. Currently, he has nine kids all between the ages of nine and fourteen. I've started to go through the process of pulling the previous foster children's files, but there are over a hundred and

## JADED

fifty of them."

"Shit," I said, shocked that it was that many.

I didn't really know much about Jasper's fostering situation. I knew he was forty-eight and he and Dana, his wife, had been married for twenty years or so, now. I knew they were foster parents, but I had never actually met any of the kids. I've never been over to his house. Whenever we'd met after work, it was at a bar or a restaurant for a meal. He didn't have photos of them. He didn't talk about them. I figured he was just a private person. We were partners, but that didn't mean we had to share every single detail of our lives with each other. He didn't even know about Shane.

"It's going to take some time to pull

## EVIE RILEY

all of their files and go through them to see if any doctor reports were made after their time with Jasper. Some were also moved to another city or out of state and I don't have access to their files," Isaiah continued.

"I can get 'em. I just need their names and I can pull the file, no matter where they were placed in the country. We need to do a sneak and peek at Jasper's house and see what is going on. I'm assuming you are operating under the impression that Jasper is cooking drugs in the house," Mason asked.

"Last night, I looked through twenty files. Twelve of the kids were admitted to the hospital with withdrawal-like symptoms. Not all of them were given blood work, most were told it was the flu and they would feel better in a few days.

## JADED

It's enough for me to make the hypothesis that cocaine is being either cooked at the house around the children, or the children were weighing and packaging the cocaine." Isaiah looked thoroughly disgusted as he relayed the information.

"That sounds like a reasonable hypothesis. I've never noticed any problems with Jasper being sick, though, in the three years he's been my partner," I stated.

It wasn't that I doubted his assumption, it did sound like something was definitely going on in that house, but I also figured Jasper and Dana would have to be sick as well.

"Depends. I've gone into a lot of homes where the drugs were made in the basement and the kids were sick but

## EVIE RILEY

the foster parents weren't. The kids were the ones touching the drugs and breathing it in as they were either cooking or packaging it, while the parents were fine, because the ventilation system in the upstairs of the house was solid. It kept the fumes down in the basement and when they needed to go down there, they wore the proper protection. It's completely logical that Jasper isn't breathing it in. Just like it's logical that he is breathing it in, but he's never not been around it. His body could be addicted to it and he gets his fix by being in the house," Mason pointed out.

That could be true.

I had never seen any signs, but I hadn't known him for twenty years. His temper could be a side effect from the drugs in his system. Big city police get

# JADED

random drug tests, but they don't do that here. They only do drug testing if the Captain thinks you are on drugs. That's never happened yet, and apparently hasn't in the last ten years. There were stories about a previous patrol officer twelve years ago that was fired for being a pothead. That was it, though.

"Let's get the files and go through them. See which kids were hospitalized after leaving Jasper's. I'll loop in Captain Perry so he's aware of the situation. We'll need to do a sneak and peek at his house. Mase, can you get a warrant from a judge? We gotta keep that out of town." There was no way we could do that here.

"I'll get it. With the files we'll have enough for a warrant," Mason said confidently.

## EVIE RILEY

"Okay, I have to go to the office and start pulling them. Do you want to join me there, or do you want me to bring them back here?" Isaiah asked.

"It would be better to do it here. We don't know who might talk to who. I want to try and keep this as quiet as possible," I answered.

Small towns and their rumor mills.

All it would take is for someone to see Isaiah grabbing the wrong file and it would be all over town that he was pulling files and looking into something. The very last thing I wanted was to tip Jasper off.

"I'll be back in about an hour or so, then," Isaiah said, before he finished his coffee and headed out.

"I'll grab my bag and get my laptop out of it. I'll get A.S.A Crawford up to

## JADED

speed and he'll grab us a warrant."

"Not exactly the vacation you were looking for. I'm sorry."

"It's okay. The drug cases are the easiest. Have you thought about just asking Tyler again? Tell him you know that Jasper could be mixed up with drugs."

It would be very logical for me to ask Tyler. Hell, he was there, why not get a first person perspective on the matter? The thought of bringing him into this, though, had my stomach up in knots. I didn't want something to happen to him. Even if he did tell me and didn't blow it off or clam up, he could be at risk if Jasper suspected he started all of this. I had to protect him.

I wasn't about to lose him like I lost Shane.

## EVIE RILEY

"No, I want to keep him out of this. I don't know what is going on, but I know that when drug dealers feel threatened, they'll attack the one they feel is responsible. I don't want Tyler getting hurt. It's better to leave him in the dark."

"It's your call, I'll support you. I'll go grab my gear," Mason said with complete understanding to his voice.

Once I was alone, I let out a long breath. This was not what I had expected, but at the same time, I wasn't about to turn my head away from it. If Jasper was dirty, I was going to put him behind bars and I would save those nine children. They deserved better and I was going to make sure everyone got justice.

Especially Tyler.

# CHAPTER SEVENTEEN

Tyler

THE PAST TWO weeks had been a whirlwind. Things between Roland and me had progressed wonderfully. I was a little worried that our friendship would be compromised by our new sexual relationship. It wasn't, though. It actually made us closer and I couldn't have been happier.

## EVIE RILEY

I wasn't living in a naive world. I knew that we would have problems. We would have arguments and we would be mad at each other. That was natural in any relationship. As for now, though, I was happy to keep living in our little bubble and I was not in any hurry to pop it.

For the past two weeks we had made out again and we had progressed to actually touching each other's dicks. I had touched myself plenty of times and I'd had women touch me, but the feel of Roland's hand on me, it was addicting. I felt like a drug addict off of his touch. I constantly craved it and when he had to work late and we couldn't see each other, withdrawal would set in. I never thought I would be like this, the type of guy that always wanted to be around

## JADED

someone, but I was. My body had been starving and now it was being given an all you can eat buffet and, damn, was it eating.

Tonight, we were at my place above the bar for dinner. It was really nice being able to share domestic tasks together. I enjoyed cooking and it was good to have Roland here helping me with it. He was a good cook as well, and he apparently enjoyed it, too. It was something we could do together outside of the bedroom.

"How has work been?" I asked, once we finished eating and were relaxing on the couch.

He had been working a lot these past two weeks. I suspected he had something going on that was a pretty big deal with the amount of whispered

## EVIE RILEY

phone calls and how much time he was spending with Mason.

It wasn't just that he was spending time with his brother. That was completely normal. What made me suspect it had to do with work was how they spent their time going through files and down at the station. They weren't going out to dinner or the movies. They were working on something and I hoped he would open up to me about it, even just a little bit. I wasn't sure if he could talk about it with it being work related and him being a detective. I would never ask him to compromise a case or his ethics, but it would be nice to hear about some of his day at work. He knows about my day. Hell, he's here for the most of it. It would just be nice to know more things about him.

# JADED

"I've been working on a big case recently. I'm sure you've noticed."

"I have. I didn't want to ask, because I didn't want to pry, but you seem stressed."

"I am stressed. It's a major case and Mason has been helping me. Isaiah has as well. He's a friend of mine that works with Social Services in the Child Protection Division. This case is very sensitive and we have to be extremely careful with how we proceed. My Captain, Captain Perry, is the only one other than me in the department that knows about this case. I've been trying to not bring it home with me, to not involve you, and it's not because I don't trust you or anything like that. I just didn't want to drag you into it. If people knew you were involved, it could be

# EVIE RILEY

dangerous, and the last thing I want is for you to be hurt."

I didn't want to be hurt, either, and I could tell how terrified he was at the prospect of me being hurt. He had lost the man he loved already due to a drunk driver. He didn't want me to suffer the same fate. He didn't love me. I knew it was too soon for that. It didn't matter that I was already falling for him, too soon or not. My heart wasn't listening to me on the matter. He might not love me, but he did care for me, and it would hurt him if I was seriously hurt or killed. I reached out and placed my hand on his thigh as I spoke.

"I know you don't want me to get hurt and I don't want that either. But, I also don't want you to feel like you can't talk to me because of that. I know we're not

## JADED

in New York City, but your job can still be dangerous and sometimes that danger might come home. We have to be able to talk about it so I'm aware of it and can be careful. I can't avoid the landmines if I don't even know they're there, Babe."

He gave a nod and placed his hand on mine as he turned to face me.

"You're right, and if I'm being honest, I could use your help. I wanted to keep you out of this, because I knew it was going to be hard on you and the last thing I want to do is cause you pain of any kind. The case that we're working on... it's Jasper. We're investigating Jasper."

A cold dread washed over me.

Jasper, his partner, my old foster parent, the man that still haunted my

## EVIE RILEY

nightmares. I had worked hard to try and forget about him, forget about what he had done to me, to the other kids.

Why would he be investigating him?"

"For what?" I managed to get out.

"The way you reacted to seeing him and how he was about mentioning he was your foster father for two years, well, it just didn't sit right with me. I asked Isaiah to look into it and see if there was something there. He discovered a lot, including that you were addicted to cocaine at fourteen."

I went to open my mouth to say something, but he cut me off before I could even form any words.

"I know you weren't a drug addict. There are a hundred and seventy-five foster kids that they've had within the past eighteen years and out of them we

## JADED

can prove that a hundred and eight of them were addicted to drugs after they left Jasper's home. Others could have been sick, but were never taken to the hospital. Mason was going to use a judge outside of the city to get a warrant to look in Jasper's house, but due to Jasper being a detective the judge wants more proof first. What we have isn't substantial, because any lawyer could argue the statistics of foster children being addicted to drugs. What we need is a witness, one of the foster children to speak up and be willing to go on record about what was happening in that house. We've reached out to some, but none are willing to do that. Isaiah is working on trying to find new homes for the nine children that are currently in Jasper's home, but it's hard to move

## EVIE RILEY

them without any legal reason to."

I slid my hand out of his and got up. I needed to move. I couldn't sit still right now, not with my mind racing like it was.

They knew about the drugs.

I didn't think anyone would ever find out about that. With Jasper being a detective, he knew how to cover his tracks, how to work around the system that he played in. No one ever suspected he was doing anything wrong, even the social workers that came into the house. They never suspected anything. But maybe the difference was Roland wasn't a small town detective or social worker. He was from a massive city and he knew what signs to look for. He had to trust his gut in the field and that instinct was still strong in him.

## JADED

It didn't surprise me that no one would talk. They all knew better.

I knew better.

You kept your mouth shut no matter how many years it'd been. It's like fight club, you don't talk about fight club. We don't talk about what happened in that house. All we'd had was each other. It didn't even matter if you were in the house at the same time, we still were there for each other.

When I got to leave at fourteen, I had met another boy when I was seventeen who had just left Jasper's house. He was really sick and I knew what it was from. I was there with him for the whole two weeks as his body went through withdrawal. It didn't matter that we didn't go through Jasper's house at the same time, all that mattered was we had

## EVIE RILEY

and we were both lucky enough to survive. Roland had no idea just how bad it was.

How bad it *is*.

He would never find anyone that would be willing to talk. I wasn't stupid, though, because if no one talked, then Jasper couldn't be shut down and he would be free to keep doing this. To keep hurting children until he eventually died. He was only forty-eight. He could go on doing this for another thirty-five years. That's thirty-five years of more pain, more children being hurt, killed, sick, and abused.

Nothing changes unless someone speaks up.

I let out a shaky breath as I leaned my back against the kitchen counter. I didn't want to be the one that spoke up,

## JADED

but I couldn't continue to be the one that stayed quiet and let another child be hurt or killed.

All of the times growing up I wished someone would storm through that door and save us. I dreamed about it. About the cops that would bust the door down and finally stop Jasper. I knew those nine kids in that house currently were feeling the same. They were waiting every minute of every day for someone to come and save them.

And here Roland was trying to just that. He was armed and ready to kick the door down. All he needed was for someone to be brave enough to speak up.

To tell their story and face the monster, once and for all.

"Pull out your phone and turn on the

## EVIE RILEY

recorder."

"Baby, no," he said as he shot to his feet and came over to me.

"I wasn't telling you this so you would talk about it. I just wanted for you to know in case something happened and Jasper mentioned something to you. It's not safe for you to be going up against him."

"And you'll protect me by arresting him. It's more than just drugs, it's more than what you know. I was trapped there for two years and all I wanted more than anything in the world was for someone to storm in and stop him. And that is exactly what those nine kids want right now and that can't happen if no one talks. The others won't talk, because there's no one there to protect them, but I have you and I know you will get him.

## JADED

Let me help you get him. Let me help you free those kids."

There was fear in his eyes and I couldn't blame him for it. I was terrified, too. Within the fear, though, I could see he was proud of me. He was proud that I was going to stand up to Jasper, stand up for those kids. If it wasn't for the fact that he did have children currently in his home, I might not have said anything. I might have taken this to my grave, but he *did* have children and he would continue to have them.

I had to stop the cycle before more children were ruined.

"Okay, but if you need to take a break, just say the word. I'll record the conversation and sometimes I'll have to ask questions if I need more details. But if you can't handle it, then tell me and

## EVIE RILEY

we can stop."

I simply gave a nod and he took my hand and guided me over to the couch once again. We sat down and I let out a shaky breath as he pulled out his cell phone and hit the record button. He said his name, the date, time, and his detective badge number before he gave a nod to me and I started to tell my story.

A story I never thought I would ever talk about.

"I was twelve when I was placed in Jasper's home. I was there just over two years before being transferred to another one at his request. He stated that I was getting to be too problematic and he was worried about the younger children. The second the social worker left me there, Jasper made sure I knew the rules. I was used to having *the talk*. Every foster

## JADED

parent did it. I had gotten good at following the rules, no matter what they were. If you followed them and didn't make any trouble or too much noise, the foster parents would leave you alone."

"What were Jasper's rules?"

"You don't do anything that causes attention. So, no fights at school, no skipping school, all marks had to be kept hidden. You never talk about what happens in the house. Unless addressed, you don't talk to him or Dana. We learned that also meant no talking around them. You eat once a day before school and if you missed it, you had to wait until the next day. He always said he wasn't going to be poor because we kept eating. No complaining, and you do as you are told when you are told to do it, no matter what it was. You break the rules, you get punished and the level of punishment would depend on how bad the violation was."

"Could you give me an example of some of the punishments either you went through or saw happen?" he asked in a gentle voice.

"He would lock us in this crawl space under the back deck. It didn't matter what the weather was like, you were in it for hours. One time, he put me in it for three days in the middle of winter. I was only in a shirt and pants and socks. There was no food or water. I used to catch the snow that fell through the slats of the deck boards and eat it for water. He hit us everyday, always where a shirt or pants would keep it hidden. Sometimes, he would use a belt or Dana would use a frying pan. The worst was

# JADED

when one of the kids would disappear."

"Disappear? What do you mean by that?"

"If one of us became too much of a problem, or a liability, Jasper would make them disappear. You could normally tell when something horrible was going to happen. He would get this look in his eyes and he would get really quiet. Me and the older kids would always make sure the younger ones were kept hidden away when that happened. He would grab the kid later on and that would be the last time anyone saw them." I sucked in a breath.

"I snuck out one night to see what was going on with Sammy. He was just nine and he almost started a fire by mistake. He dropped a chemical. It was an accident but Jasper was furious. I

## EVIE RILEY

saw a man with Jasper. He handed over a wad of cash and took Sammy. Jasper did that about twenty times in the two years I was there." I twisted my fingers together, the memories pushing my anxiety up.

"A few times, though, one of the kids would do something that Jasper saw as unforgivable. The kid would be grabbed at night and we could hear screaming and then it got really quiet. In the morning, there would be blood on the floor, a big pool of it, and we were told to clean it up. No one ever saw the kid again. Jasper used to threaten us about putting us with the Forgotten Kids, that's what he called them."

I wiped my cheeks as the tears started to come down. I had never talked about this before, not with anyone. We

## JADED

didn't talk about it, especially the Forgotten Kids. None of us wanted to be one of them, so we always did what we could. We always went above and beyond our duty just to avoid it. All of the older kids would protect the younger ones and make sure they didn't lag behind. We always hit our quota, no matter what, because we knew that anyone of us could be added to the Forgotten Kids list, and that would be on us.

Roland reached out and took my hand in his as he spoke. "Do you know where he might have buried the kids?"

"No, he never said. And he didn't really say anything about the kids that were taken in the middle of the night. But Dana and him were arguing one night and I heard them. She was upset

## EVIE RILEY

that they weren't getting more per kid. Said they should start getting younger kids because they go for a higher price. Jasper said you can't guarantee a younger kid won't talk, that it was better to stick with nine and up."

"Okay, can you tell me how you got the cocaine into your system when you were fourteen?"

That was the easiest part to talk about. I wasn't happy about it, and it was horrible going through the withdrawal. I was sick for two weeks and completely on my own. I spent it on the bathroom floor curled up just waiting to die, essentially. My current foster parents didn't care. The father would just walk over me and use the bathroom as if I was a floor mat. He had actually stepped on me plenty of times because I

## JADED

was in his way.

"In the basement there's a lab where we were to cook the cocaine, weigh it, and package it. We didn't have gloves or anything to protect us from it. The whole basement had some type of venting system, though, because it was loud. The older kids said it was to protect the rest of the house from the fumes. We worked in the basement from the moment we got home from school until two in the morning. On weekends, we would work all day and night. When the shipment was ready, we would get into his van and drive to other towns around us and deliver the packages to different drug dealers. We had a set quota to fill each week and we made sure we always hit it. If we didn't, we would all be punished. Me and the older kids would

## EVIE RILEY

sometimes stay awake for three days straight to give the younger kids the chance to rest. We made masks for them out of what we could salvage from around the house to try and protect them from the fumes."

"Why didn't you ever say anything? To a teacher, to your social worker, or to your next foster parents?"

I knew he wasn't asking in a rude way. He had to ask because people would logically assume I would have told someone. The thing was, they didn't grow up in the foster system. Any foster child would tell you that you never talked about anything that happened within the walls of any house.

"Jasper made sure we all knew not to say anything. As for my social worker, he didn't care. In all the foster homes I

# JADED

had been in, they were all abusive. Teachers looked the other way. My social worker only saw me as an annoyance. The system is broken. It's been broken for decades. No one cares about foster kids. We're a burden that no one wants to truly take on. They take on foster kids for the status of it. *Look at me, I'm helping this poor child.* But when something goes wrong in their life, we're the first person they take their frustrations and anger out on. We don't matter and no one ever listens."

"I'm listening and I'm not going to let it go unnoticed or ignored any longer. Thank you, Tyler."

He closed out the recording before he turned it off and then instantly he was pulling me into his arms. Feeling the safety that surrounded me, I couldn't hold back the tears any longer. I completely broke down against his chest as the pain from the memories became too much. He didn't say anything and I appreciated that.

There was nothing he could truly say that would make me feel any better, that would make this any better. I hoped that he would be able to stop it, that he could stop Jasper, but I truly didn't know. Jasper was a cop and there was no telling what connections he had. At least it would be known, though, and hopefully that would save some children.

"I'm so proud of you, Baby," he said, and pressed a kiss to my head as my sobs finally started to calm down.

"It was really bad."

"I know. I'm so sorry you had to go through that. He can't hurt you anymore. I'm not going to let him. I'm not going to let him get away with what he's done and he's never going to hurt another child again. This is what we needed to arrest him. Thank you for being brave and telling me this."

"Just get him, okay?"

"I will. I promise." He kissed my head once again and I could feel my body getting weaker. I was hitting a wall and I really needed to get some sleep.

"Will you stay with me tonight?" I asked as I moved back so I could see him.

"Of course. Come on, you get ready for bed and I'll clean up. Then, we can curl up in bed together."

I gave a small nod before I got up off the couch and headed into the bathroom. I needed a minute to try and

## EVIE RILEY

get my thoughts and breathing back under control. I thought maybe I would feel better after talking about it, but I just felt heavy and exhausted. Hopefully, some sleep would do me some good and tomorrow I wouldn't wake up feeling like complete shit.

# CHAPTER EIGHTEEN

Tyler

THE LOUD BANG of thunder instantly had me sitting up and breathing heavy. The apartment was filled with the sound of rain hitting the window and the stairs out back. Thunderstorms were something I was not very good with. I hated them, always had, since I was a little kid. I couldn't help the flinch at the

## EVIE RILEY

feeling of hands on my arms.

"Hey, it's okay. It's just me, Baby."

"Sorry, I hate thunderstorms."

"Come here."

Roland pulled me down and tucked me against his chest. I instantly curled up against his heat, soothed by the sound of his heart thrumming under my ear as he held me tightly.

His arms were so big, but they made me feel safe. I never thought I would feel safe in his arms due to the size of him, but I did. He felt amazing and for the first time in my life, I felt truly safe. I never wanted that feeling to disappear. I wanted to stay in his arms forever, in this safe bubble where nothing could hurt me. I flinched at another loud crack and rumble and he ran his hand up and down my back as he spoke.

## JADED

"When I was eighteen, on my birthday, I was on the bus to boot camp. Boot camp was only six weeks, so I was placed in the infantry division and sent on tour three months later. We were all told what it would be like, we all knew that we were walking into a war zone, but seeing it and hearing about it were two different things. I thought I was fine with it, but then two weeks into my six month tour, the base was attacked in the middle of the night. Suddenly, there were bombs going off around the outside perimeter and gunfire was echoing throughout the night. We were in the barracks when it started and the guys all got up, threw their boots on, and were out of there. But me, I was frozen. All I could focus on were the bangs from the explosions. A soldier that had been

## EVIE RILEY

in for five years came over to me and told me to count the seconds in between the blasts, to focus on the seconds. It helped me to calm down and I was able to go out there and join in on the fight. I kept counting, though, and I knew that when the blasts got longer in between, that meant it was almost over. When I got back from my tour, that first thunderstorm scared the hell out of me. I snapped out of bed and grabbed my gun thinking I was still on base. It took me a minute to realize that I was at home and it was merely thunder. The only way I could relax was to count the time in between the booms."

I liked it when he shared pieces about his time either in the army or when he was in New York. He was older than me and he'd had a life before we met, before

# JADED

he got in town. It was nice to hear him share those pieces with me.

"The further the time in between, the further away the storm is," I said with understanding.

"Exactly. You're safe, Baby. I promise I'm not going to let anything happen to you."

"I know. I still don't like thunder," I said with a soft smile against his chest.

He rolled us over so he was on top of me as he spoke. "Let's see what we can do to change that."

"I like that idea."

I couldn't help but grin as he wiggled himself between my legs and closed the gap between our lips. Now this was a much better way to get through a thunderstorm. We had our own storm approaching and I hoped that we would

## EVIE RILEY

make it through. We were stronger together. I believed that with everything in me, and I knew with Roland by my side we would get through any storm that tried to take us out.

# CHAPTER NINETEEN

Roland

"ALL RIGHT, I got the no knock warrant," Mason said as he walked into the tactical room.

I had been there getting ready with Captain Perry. Isaiah had arrived a few minutes ago as well. This morning, I had come straight into work to speak with Mason and Captain Perry about what

## EVIE RILEY

Tyler had told me last night. I played the recording for them and I could instantly see how furious they were. I could understand it perfectly. I wanted blood myself.

When we started this, when *I* started this, I thought maybe Jasper had let his anger get the better of him and he had hurt Tyler. I never expected to discover he could be involved in drugs, and now, we not only knew he was involved in producing and distributing drugs, but he had killed children and sold them. He was far more dangerous than any of us ever knew and we had to be ready for anything.

It was why Mason went with the recording and personally delivered it to his judge friend in Baltimore. He had called me an hour ago, letting me know

## JADED

he was on his way back with the warrant.

Captain Perry had rounded up everyone that we had at the station, all ten detectives, to go and make the arrest on Jasper and Dana. What they didn't know was that they were arresting one of their own. It was going to be a problem and I knew most wouldn't want to believe it or be involved. They wouldn't have a choice, though, with Captain Perry giving the orders.

I wasn't sure how this was going to go over, I really wasn't. I knew the blue line was extremely important and cherished by every cop within the country. You didn't go against the blue brotherhood, even if that meant keeping quiet about a dirty cop. For the most part, I went along with it. I was not about to go through the

## EVIE RILEY

headache of trying to get a cop fired for taking bribes to look the other way on tickets or even drug dealers.

In New York, there was no point because once you got one drug dealer off the street, five more took their place. I had learned that it was better to deal with the devils you knew then get some hotheaded moron that just wanted to drop bodies on the streets.

But we weren't talking about a shady cop letting drug dealers off. What Jasper was doing was putting children, innocent children, at risk. He was having them making cocaine and selling it. He was abusing them, starving them, selling them, and killing them. That wasn't something I would stand for. I wasn't about to stand by and let that continue. I didn't care who I pissed off in the

## JADED

process. If the guys that worked here didn't like it, then, as far as I was concerned, they didn't need to work here and I knew Captain Perry felt the same.

"We brief everyone in ten," Captain Perry said before he turned on his heel and strode out the door.

"Grab whatever you need," I said to my brother, gesturing to the supply table, knowing he didn't come down here with all of his tactical gear.

He gave a nod and headed over to grab a vest and one of the tactical long guns as Isaiah spoke.

"What about Koda?"

"I'll bring him with me so he can help with the children. We have no idea what the kids are going to be like. Do you have transport for the children?" Mason responded as he started to get ready.

## EVIE RILEY

"I have a fellow social worker on standby with a van to transport the children to the hospital. I haven't found new placements yet, though. I need to see what their medical conditions are like and if they have any cocaine in their systems first. Chances are they will and they'll need to stay in the hospital for at least a week. What about the other children, though? The ones that were sold. We can't just forget about them."

That was going to be the trickier part, because unless Dana or Jasper talked, we would have no idea where they were. It would take time to try and track anyone down. We would need to go through all of Jasper's finances, emails, phone calls, everything to see if something stood out and if it didn't, we would be at a dead end.

## JADED

"I've already contacted my boss about the situation down here. He wants me to stay here and build a task force to track down the missing children and make sure the foster system down here is safe for every child within it. Looks like you and I are going to be around each other for a while yet," Mason said to Isaiah.

"I'm happy to have the help and I'm more than willing to help in any way that I can," Isaiah easily agreed and flashed a warm smile.

He was going to need all the help he could get. Trying to rework a system that had been functioning this way for decades was going to be one hell of an undertaking.

Each foster home, past and present, would need to be investigated to ensure no wrongdoing to any child. It wasn't going to be easy and it was going to take a lot of time.

At the same time, though, I was happy that Mason would be here longer. I was worried about him and not just what this job was doing to him. He seemed jumpy, on edge, like he was waiting for an attack. That wasn't like him. Something more was going on with him and I was going to get to the bottom of it. First, we had to take care of Jasper, and then he and I would be having that discussion.

"Who's heading the task force?" I asked as we finished grabbing the last of our gear.

"I am. My boss is putting me in charge and allowing me to pick who I want on it from Homeland, local police and a child protective worker liaison. I

## JADED

assumed, Isaiah, you'd wish to be that liaison."

"Yes, I would. Thank you."

"You better be placing me on that team," I said with a knowing smirk.

I knew I would be. There was no way my little brother would be running a task force and not have me as his secondhand man. I was very proud of him. He was getting to run his own task force. This was huge and it would be an amazing career opportunity for him. He had worked his ass off from the ground up and his boss clearly noticed his skills and potential.

"Wouldn't think otherwise. Let's go get this bastard," Mason said as he put the clip into his gun.

We all headed out and crowded into the small briefing room that also worked as the roll call room. This place was very small and I couldn't imagine being able to house a task force. Mason would need to figure out where to put up his new team while they were setting up shop in town. This station would not be able to hold them. Not to mention, we didn't have anywhere near the computer power they would need to run their investigation.

Captain Perry was already in the room. He stood at the front, ready and waiting for us. We moved over to the side of the room to give Captain Perry our full attention.

We were operating on everyone not knowing that I had started the investigation into Jasper. It would be better, for now, if people believed the Captain had been looking into it. When

## JADED

he had told me he was going to play down my role in all of this, I wasn't happy about it. Not because of glory or recognition, I could care less about that. It was about him feeling like I should have to hide what I was doing.

I didn't want to hide behind someone.

I didn't need to.

I had gone up against a lot worse than anyone in this building. I didn't shy away from terrorist cells. I was not about to give Jasper that privilege. Still, he was my Captain and I firmly believed in following the chain of command, so I kept quiet and focused on being a silent support.

"Before we begin, I want to make one thing very clear. This is *not* a training exercise. You are the more experienced detectives that I have. Some of you have

## EVIE RILEY

never done a raid before outside of a training exercise. The majority of you have only ever done one or two raids when a nearby town needs more bodies. Due to the type of raid that we are about to go on, I am going to rely on experience to lead us. Detective Wright and his brother, Special Agent Mason Wright, will be taking point on this raid. I expect everyone to follow their orders and do as they tell you, myself included. What matters most is that we all come home alive and no one gets killed tonight. Do I make myself clear?" He paused to allow the reality of this situation to sink in.

Captain Perry was right. None of them had any real experience doing a raid. They were used to training exercises or helping out in the back on a raid. There wasn't anyone we could call

## JADED

in for this, it had to be the men in this room, and the only reason I wasn't more concerned was because Mason was standing next to me. He would be able to handle anything that we come across in that house.

I quickly scanned the room to see everyone's reactions. Some were concerned and worried about just what we were about to do. Others seemed excited at finally being able to do something active on the job. My gaze traveled over to Baxter. I wasn't really happy that he was here. It wasn't that he was a dirty cop or anything, just a lazy and bigoted one. He was also close with Jasper and I wasn't too sure he would believe what we were saying about him. He could be problematic, but we didn't have much choice right now.

## EVIE RILEY

Next to Baxter stood his partner. Jarod. He stood behind him slightly and looked very uncomfortable. He was a younger guy, but he had a lot of potential. When I got into town, he was a rookie patrol officer, but he wasn't content to just sit around a desk all day. He was out there on the streets talking to people, watching them and getting involved. He was always reading a book. Sometimes it was on forensic science, profiling, criminal law, federal law, and even negotiation tactics. This kid was always learning and I suspected he had a higher IQ then he allowed others to see. He wasn't timid, but he was shy and didn't tend to speak up. He seemed a bit apprehensive with people. Even after the past few years, I still didn't know anything about him personally. He had

## JADED

managed to impress Captain Perry a year ago with his work ethic so much so that the Captain had promoted him to detective and partnered him up with Baxter.

The two of them didn't click at all and I had been considering asking the Captain to switch our partners. Jarod seemed to want to learn, but Baxter had zero interest in teaching him. It was something I might have to actually do once the dust settled on this raid.

"Keep an eye on Baxter tonight. I don't know if he'll be a team player," I whispered to Mason.

He simply gave a nod and I knew I didn't need to tell him who exactly Baxter was. He had already heard about him from me after I punched the asshat. Mason would keep an eye on him tonight

## EVIE RILEY

so I could focus on Jasper.

"We have secured a no knock warrant for the home of one of our own. Jasper Monroe. He has been under investigation for the past few weeks for suspected drug trafficking. We secured the warrant based on an eyewitness account of drugs being produced in the basement. We also have evidence of him killing foster children and selling them to pedophiles for close to two decades. We have an arrest warrant for Jasper and his wife Dana," Captain Perry continued.

"You expect us to believe that one of our own, that a cop who has almost thirty years on the job, is not only a drug dealer, but a child killer? Who is this eyewitness, Santa Claus?" Baxter asked, clearly not believing anything Captain Perry had to say.

## JADED

I knew he wasn't going to believe it. I could see the doubt in almost everyone's eyes. Interestingly enough, I didn't see doubt in Jarod's eyes.

"Why doesn't the kid seem surprised?" Mason whispered to me. Apparently, I wasn't the only one who had noticed.

"That's Jarod Lopez. He's Baxter's partner. He's only been a detective for a year, but he joined the police force at eighteen. He's only twenty-one and has a shit load of potential. But I don't know anything about him. He keeps everything personal under wraps. He's smart, though. Smarter than he wants people to know. He could have easily seen something," I whispered back.

"The witness' identity is being kept a secret, for obvious reasons. We have

## EVIE RILEY

more than enough evidence to back up the claims. Once we get into the house, we'll find the lab in his basement. He currently has nine foster children that we will need to ensure are safe before they are transported to the hospital for evaluations. Due to the nature of this investigation, all cell phones will be left here in the station. I don't want anyone reaching out to either Jasper or Dana. Agent Wright, you wished to say something," Captain Perry said with a pointed look at Mason.

Mason moved to stand at the front of the room and I was hit with a strong sense of pride once more. He was so confident in himself and it warmed my heart. I was a proud big brother and I couldn't wait for him to be around more. It was going to be really good for the

## JADED

both of us.

"Due to the connection Jasper has to this police department, his charges will be placed by Homeland Security, making them federal charges. He will be eligible for the death penalty, which means anyone that tries to contact him or help him in any way will be charged with aiding and abetting a wanted criminal, as well as an accessory after the fact. You will be facing hard time in a federal prison, and I will personally ensure you are placed within general population and not solitary." He paused to allow the seriousness of the situation to sink in before he continued.

"We are going to hit his home in two teams. Roland's team will hit the front door and my team will hit the back and hold down the perimeter. Once the

## EVIE RILEY

arrests have been made, Isaiah will then handle the children. If you cannot do your job, then speak up now, because once we leave you will have no choice but to do your job and ensure that Jasper does not evade arrest."

You heard him, does anyone want to be kept here?" Captain Perry asked.

I waited to see someone raise their hand, but surprisingly no one did. They weren't happy, but they were riding with us. Nothing more needed to be said, so we all got divided up into the two teams and once we dropped our phones off into the basket, we headed out.

The drive up to Jasper's house was done in silence. There was nothing anyone could say and we were all on edge. The guys weren't happy about arresting one of their own, especially a

## JADED

veteran with almost thirty years on the job. It wasn't a good situation to be in and I understood that. I wouldn't want to be here, either, and I might not believe the evidence if I was in their position. They would believe it, though, once they saw the lab. Once they saw the kids in that house. I just hoped everything went smoothly tonight.

The convoy of police vehicles pulled up to the house as one. We all got out of our vehicles and instantly made our way into position with our respective teams. Mason ran around the back of the house and when he was ready, he gave me a nod to go ahead. A quick look over at my Captain, who gave me a simple nod, and I kicked down the door.

We ran in with our guns up and ready for anything. I wasn't even in for

## EVIE RILEY

two seconds when the backdoor was kicked in and Mason came into the house. He had three guys in the back and I had three in the front holding the perimeter. As we all made our way through the main level of the house and then up the stairs, we quickly discovered that the house was quieter then we expected. It wasn't until we reached the bedroom when we found Dana in bed on her laptop with headphones in that we understood. Now it made sense why she didn't hear us. I easily went over and once I was close enough, she looked up and promptly screamed.

"Put your hands up," I ordered, not even bothering with lowering my gun.

"What are you doing here?" she demanded as she removed her headphones.

## JADED

"Dana Monroe you're under arrest for crimes against children and drug trafficking. Get your hands up," I ordered, keeping my voice sharp so she knew I wasn't playing around.

"Are you out of your mind, Roland? You know me. You know *us*. We're not criminals."

She wasn't going to make this easy on me and that was just fine by me. I looked over and saw that Jarod was in the room with me and he had his gun trained on her. I lowered mine and grabbed her, pulling her out of the bed and slamming her face first into the floor before cuffing her. After reading her her rights, which she yelled and screamed at me throughout, I dragged her to her feet as Mason's voice came over the comms.

"House is cleared. Jasper isn't here."

## EVIE RILEY

"Fuck," I said under my breath as I headed out of the bedroom with Dana.

As we made our way toward the front door, I noticed that Isaiah was already being escorted into the house and they were starting to round up the children. I brought Dana out to one of the cars and tossed her into the backseat.

"Where is he?" I demanded.

"He went away for a boy's weekend. It was a surprise for him. He's going to be pissed when he comes back home to find out you arrested me. Your career is over, Roland."

"The only career that is ruined is his. But don't worry, we have a very nice ten by ten cell with your name on it."

I slammed the door and ordered one of my guys to drive her back to the station and process her. I made a direct

## JADED

order for no one to talk to her or let her call or talk to anyone.

"Apparently, he's away on a surprise boys' weekend," I told Mason and Captain Perry once I reached the house.

"Bullshit," Mason instantly said.

"He's up to something. You think he caught wind of the investigation?" Captain Perry asked.

"Someone who has almost thirty years of experience on the job holds a lot of connections. There's no telling who he could have heard something from. Could have been someone within social services. It would make sense that he had a mole on the inside. Someone that could feed him the children that no one would think twice about when they went missing. Someone to help cover it all up. He could have been made aware of the investigation once files started to be pulled," Mason stated.

"Shit. And now he's in the wind," I said as I shook my head.

We should have seen this coming. *I* should have seen this coming. Of course Jasper had connections within our department and social services. He grew up here. He would have known everyone in that damn building. He had been planning his escape for weeks now and he left Dana here to take the fall for it all.

"Detective Wright, sir," Jarod said with uncertainty in his voice. He was clearly nervous about walking in on our conversation, but he seemed determined to do it. He clutched a folded up piece of paper in his hand and he spoke as he held it out to me.

## JADED

"One of the children said he was told to give this to you."

"What is it?" Captain Perry asked as I grabbed the paper.

As I opened it, the words on the page brought a cold dread to flood my entire body.

*It's your fault for him breaking the rules. Dead men tell no tales, Wright.*

"Roland, what is it?" Mason asked, now on edge.

"Tyler," I said, before I turned and bolted for my car.

Mason climbed into my passenger seat, slamming the door closed as I gunned the motor and slammed the car into gear simultaneously. The tires spun for a moment before catching the pavement and, in seconds, we were rocketing down the street.

## EVIE RILEY

Jasper was going after Tyler, after the man that I was falling in love with. I wasn't going to allow that to happen. I wasn't going to lose another man that I loved.

Not tonight. Not again.

# CHAPTER TWENTY

Tyler

DRAINED.

Completely and utterly drained seemed like the best way, the only way, to describe how I felt tonight. Between the thunderstorm and telling Roland my story, I did not sleep well. Having to get up this morning was a Herculean effort, one I wasn't certain I would be able to

## EVIE RILEY

pull off.

Roland had been very sweet this morning, though. He had made me breakfast in bed before he had to head out for work. I knew he had to get the recording in so he could get a warrant, but I appreciated him taking the time to make breakfast and spend the time with me.

I spent the rest of the day hanging around the apartment before going down to the bar for my shift. Tonight had been busy, which was nice to make the time go by faster, but it left me feeling even more exhausted. It had died down for the past hour with it being a weeknight. It was so dead, I had sent Tammy home and Jose had closed the kitchen so he could head home, too. It was just me in an empty bar, something that was odd

## JADED

but also nice. It allowed me to start doing the cleaning and getting things ready for when I could close.

I checked my phone to see if Roland had sent me any texts. I knew he was stressed and busy working tonight, but I wasn't sure if he would have the time to send me a text and check in with me. I wouldn't hold it against him if he didn't. He was busy trying to get Jasper in jail and I knew that was not going to be easy at all. I hoped to be able to see him tonight so I knew that he was okay.

"What the hell is that?"

There was a clicking sound coming from somewhere. I thought I had heard it a few minutes ago, but with the traffic on the street that often sounded through the walls, I blew it off. Now, though, I was certain something was clicking.

## EVIE RILEY

Moving around the back of the bar, I looked to see if there was something back there that would be clicking.

It sounded like an old school clock where the second hand ticked as it moved around the clock. The thing was, there was no analog clock behind the bar and I couldn't find anything that would be clicking. It was just liquor bottles and glasses along the back of the bar. There weren't any electronics and the cash register wouldn't click. I couldn't find a reason for something to be making a random noise.

All of a sudden the clicking stopped.

The eerie silence rang out in the bar for a split second, and then pain exploded across my chest.

The world faded in and out all around me. I fought to keep my eyes open, but

# JADED

all I could see was fog. I couldn't seem to clear the fog away, everything was blurry.

Something was wrong.

I knew I needed to do something, but I couldn't seem to get my mind to function enough to tell me what I needed to do. I could hear a loud alarm going off. At least, I hoped it was an alarm and not my ears. I closed my eyes again and this time I couldn't seem to bring myself to open them.

I took the time to attempt to figure out what was going on, but for the life of me I couldn't. I took inventory of my body and focused on my other senses. My body ached and it felt like something pressed on my back. I could feel the cold floor underneath me, my shirt wet with what smelled like gin.

## EVIE RILEY

A coughing fit suddenly overwhelmed me and, to my horror, I couldn't seem to get a decent breath in. My chest felt tight, constricted. I couldn't get my lungs to expand and a fire raged within my chest. It felt like an asthma attack but worse. It hurt like hell each time I gasped in my desperate need for air and my throat burned.

I forced my eyes open, only to have to shut them as they started to burn and water. In that split second I noticed there was smoke. Black smoke, billowing throughout the bar, filling it up and sucking out the remaining oxygen at a rapid pace. I could hear more than just the alarm going off, I could hear the roar of a fire.

*The bar is on fire.*

The clicking, it must have been from

## JADED

a bomb or something.

I had to move. I couldn't stay here. Forcing myself to get up turned out to be a lot harder than I expected it to be. I couldn't get up, there was something heavy across my back. I was stuck until someone came to help me lift whatever was on me.

Another coughing fit shook my body and it left me fighting even harder for a breath. It became harder and harder to breathe, to not choke on the smoke. My vision kept going in and out. I could feel myself getting weaker. I could feel the heat of the flames becoming hotter, creeping closer to me.

I suddenly realized what it meant that I was lying in liquor. If the flames got too close, I would be on fire along with the bar. I had to get up, but I couldn't lift

## EVIE RILEY

the weight off of me. The back of the bar must have fallen on top of me and it was a good three hundred pounds so it could hold up the liquor bottles.

The world was starting to get darker, but before I could sink into the blackness, I heard the rapid barks of a dog. It was random and for a second I thought I imagined it, until a very wet tongue ran up my cheek. I forced my eyes to open and sure enough there was a large dog in front of me.

"Roland, over here!" A male voice called out from my left.

I wasn't sure who it was or who he was calling, but someone was here. They could get help. They could get me out of here before I barbecued. I was losing the fight with the darkness once again, but then the sweetest sounding voice I had

## JADED

ever heard in my life dragged me back to consciousness.

"Ty! Baby, can you hear me?"

"Help me lift this," the first man said.

I could hear Roland and whoever was with him shuffling and suddenly the weight disappeared. I felt teeth around my wrist before I was being pulled away from whatever had pinned me to the ground.

*The dog.*

The dog was pulling me free and once I was far enough away he let me go. The world spun and by the time it cleared, I was up in Roland's arms and we were running out of the building. Even the fresh air wasn't enough for me to be able to breathe properly. For some reason, it made my breathing worse as another coughing fit overcame me, one that had me feeling weak and on the verge of passing out.

"Medics!" Roland yelled, and again the world passed me by in a blur as I fought to catch my breath.

Something was wrong.

I couldn't catch my breath. I couldn't get a proper breath even though we were outside in the crisp night air. My chest was still on fire. It was tight and burned. I needed it to stop. I needed to breathe.

Roland's arms were suddenly gone and I was on something soft with blurry strangers standing over me. Everything was blurry and spinning. I couldn't make it stop. They were talking to me, I could see their mouths moving, but I couldn't hear them.

I couldn't hear anything.

Everything was fading, the blackness

## JADED

at the corner of my eyes was moving in, threatening to swallow me whole. They were panicking, I could see it in their eyes, by the looks they were giving to each other.

Roland was scared.

I wanted to tell him it would be okay, but I couldn't get the words to form before everything went black.

# CHAPTER TWENTY-ONE

Roland

SITTING IN A hard plastic hospital chair next to a hospital bed that contained the man that I loved was the hardest thing I had ever done in my life.

When we arrived at the bar and saw that it was up in flames, my heart tried to escape my body through my mouth. I thought I would actually throw up and

## EVIE RILEY

my heart would be on the ground.

Thank God Mason was with me and had reacted so quickly. I was right behind him, but him flying into the burning building without thought or care for his own safety was what snapped me out of my complete terror. When we found Tyler in the middle of all of those flames, I thought he was dead. It wasn't until I reached him and saw that he was alive and breathing did I feel like I could catch my breath again. Only to feel like I was dying once more when it was clear he was having extreme trouble breathing. Having to stand there and watch as the paramedic shoved a tube down his throat...

Fuck, I was going to have nightmares about it for years to come.

It had been a day since Tyler had

## JADED

been admitted into the hospital. He was still intubated, but his oxygen levels were going up. The doctor was just being cautious because of Tyler's asthma. The smoke he'd inhaled aggravated his asthma and that made it harder for his lungs to function on their own. They had also been keeping him sedated so his body didn't fight the tube.

I was thankful that he was asleep right now. I couldn't imagine trying to be awake with a tube down my throat. I would be pulling it out the first chance I got. Even though the doctor said he would be okay, I wasn't going to relax until I saw for myself that Tyler would recover.

Until I could see him awake and talking again.

The door opened and I turned my

attention to see who had walked in.

"Any update?" Mason asked as he headed over to me and handed me a coffee.

"The doc isn't going to give him any more sedation. He thinks it'll be okay for him to wake up today and then he'll pull the tube out."

"Good, that's good, Bro."

"Is Koda okay?"

Koda had run into the bar before either Mason or I could even start running. He'd jumped right through the window and immediately started to search for victims. He was trained for it, but I knew Mason hated it when Koda was put in danger. Koda had been the one to find Tyler first, though, and his barking alerted Mason. The fire was all around us by then and I knew Koda's

## JADED

paws had been injured from the heat on the floor.

"He's good. A doctor checked him over for me and put some cream on the bottom of his paws. First degree burns, but in a few days he'll be okay. I've got his paws wrapped to keep from any dirt aggravating his burns. He's hanging out in the kid's playroom right now on the floor."

"You left him there?"

That surprised me. Koda always went where Mason did. Always. It didn't matter who was there, Koda always followed Mason when he left a room, even at the house.

"Jarod was there with the kids as Isaiah worked with one of the doctors. I called him, but he didn't want to follow. Apparently, he's happy to lay next to

Jarod."

I couldn't help but chuckle at that. "Maybe Koda finally sniffed out your soul mate."

He rolled his eyes in a dramatic fashion. He didn't believe in soul mates and even if he did, I doubted he would see Jarod as his. He liked smaller guys, but Jarod wasn't small. He wasn't my size, but he was equal to Mason. That right there was a no go to him. Still, they would be cute together, assuming Jarod was even gay.

"What do we know?" I asked, moving my attention back to what mattered the most.

"Well, the tests have started to come back and, so far, it's looking like all the kids are addicted to cocaine. The doc is going to keep them for at least a week,

## JADED

possibly two depending on how bad the withdrawals are. Dana has lawyered up. Apparently, she expected Jasper to come back and rescue her. Once she figured out he'd left her holding the bag, she clammed right up and yelled lawyer. I'm trying to get her denied bail, but I don't know if it'll stick. We have all of the electronics from the house and more than enough evidence of the drugs. But we still can't find him. None of the kids are talking about it. The few that have talked, all said it was Dana. That Jasper didn't even know about the drugs."

*Fuck.*

"Bullshit. It was in his basement. Of course he knew about the drugs. He's trained them to put all of the blame on his wife, like fucking a coward."

Just when I thought the man couldn't

## EVIE RILEY

go any lower, he took off and left his wife to face the full punishment for his crimes. It wasn't going to be an easy open and shut case. The case couldn't even *be* closed until they found Jasper.

"I got a BOLO out on his ID and his photo is being sent to every federal agency all across the country. I'll find him, but it might take some time. I'm going to bring Jarod onto the task force. He seems smart and like a good person. He's good with kids, which will help as we come across victims."

I doubted that was his only reasoning. I think my little brother had a crush on the young detective, but he wasn't willing to accept it yet.

"He's got potential, I think he'll do great. Once Ty is set back home, I can help you with finding Jasper."

## JADED

"You're not on the task force, Roland."

"What the fuck are you talking about?" I snapped. There was no way I wasn't going to be hunting down that son of a bitch.

"You can't be out there looking for Jasper. I know you want to, I get it, but if you are out there with me, who the hell is going to be here protecting Tyler? The only way to make a case against Jasper for multiple counts of murder and child trafficking is Tyler's testimony. Jasper knows that and he won't stop until Tyler is dead. You need to be here with him, protecting him."

He was right.

I didn't want to admit it, but he was right. Jasper was not going to stop at anything to silence Tyler. If I was out there with Mason trying to track him down, that left Tyler vulnerable to an attack. I needed to be close so I could keep an eye on him and ensure he was safe. I let out a sigh and gave a small nod in defeat. He placed a comforting hand on my shoulder as I spoke.

"I'll get him, I promise you."

I knew he would. If there was one thing my brother did better than anyone, it was hunt down monsters. He would find him and he would make sure he paid for every sin he committed.

# CHAPTER TWENTY-TWO

Roland

IT WAS NEARING nine at night when finally Tyler started showing signs of waking up. It had almost been a full two days since he had been admitted and even though the doc said he would be okay, I had a hard time believing it with how long it was taking for him to wake up. The second his hand twitch in mine,

## EVIE RILEY

I was on my feet and sitting down on the edge of the bed, making sure that Tyler would see me when he opened his eyes.

"That's it, Baby, let me see those mesmerizing eyes of yours," I said as I reached out and rubbed my thumb against his cheek.

Slowly, Tyler blinked his eyes open and I could finally see him awake. It only took a second before they were filled with confusion and panic set in. I reached over and hit the call button for the nurse as I spoke.

"It's okay. You're okay. I know it's hard, but you have to stay still. You had to be intubated from the smoke, but the doc will remove it for you. Just relax your throat and don't fight it. Let it breathe for you, Baby."

I wiped the tear that escaped from his

## JADED

eyes. He was scared, but he was listening to me and not fighting against the tube. I knew fighting it would make it worse. I didn't want him choking, because I wasn't certain I wouldn't pull the damn thing out myself if that happened. The door opened and I was thankful it was actually the doctor and not a nurse. He spoke as he made his way over to the other side of the bed.

"Good evening, Mr. Foster, it is good to see you awake. I'm Dr. Richards. I've been treating you for smoke inhalation from the fire you were in. You had to be intubated to help your lungs recover from the smoke. I'd like to remove the tube and see how your lungs handle breathing on their own. Do you understand?"

Tyler gave a very small nod and I

squeezed his hand to make sure he knew I wasn't going anywhere. I watched as Dr. Richards moved around and grabbed what he needed to get the tube out. I could see the tension in Tyler's body and I couldn't blame him. It wasn't going to be comfortable getting that tube out. Once he was ready, Dr. Richards spoke.

"I'm going to start pulling the tube out now. I need you to give deep coughs as I do, it will help relax your throat and make it easier for me to get the tube out, okay?"

Once again Tyler gave a small nod, and the doc started to pull on the tube. Tyler did as he was supposed to and coughed until the horrible tube was finally out of him. The coughing instantly got worse and I reached over to

# JADED

grab him some water.

"Small sips," Dr. Richards warned.

"Try some water, Baby." I brought the cup over to his mouth as I spoke.

I helped him take a few sips before I pulled the cup back and I was pleased that it did help to stop the coughing. Dr. Richards went on to check Tyler's breathing and listen to his chest. Neither of us spoke while the doctor worked and I was relieved when he didn't appear disappointed.

"They sound good. I want you to keep this nasal canal in for the rest of the night and, if your oxygen levels stay stable, you should be able to go home sometime tomorrow."

"Are there signs we should be looking out for?" I asked, as the doctor got Tyler set up with the oxygen line under his nose.

"The smoke will aggravate his asthma, still, so if there are any signs that it's getting worse, page a nurse. We might need to do some breathing treatments with a nebulizer to help clear his lungs out. The best thing for him right now is to sleep."

"Thanks, Doc," I said on our behalf.

"I'll be back to check in on you later on tonight," he said to Tyler before he turned on his heel and strode out the door.

Once we were alone, I instantly bent down and placed my lips against his. He weakly kissed me back and I could feel how exhausted he was. I pulled back, but stayed close so if he did talk I would be able to hear him. I ran my hand through his hair as I spoke, my voice

# JADED

thick with emotion.

"I thought I had lost you."

"I'm okay." Tyler gave me a weak smile and placed his hand on my thigh.

His voice was very raspy and raw from the tube and smoke. I hated it and wished I could have made it better for him. If there was one thing this whole experience had taught me, it was that I was madly in love with him. I wasn't falling in love, I had already fallen, hard, and it wasn't puppy love like with Shane. This was all consuming, it might kill me love and I wouldn't change it for anything.

"I love you. And I know it's too soon and I don't expect you to say it back," I started, but he cut me off with his own raspy voice.

"I love you, too."

## EVIE RILEY

He gave me a warm smile and instantly I smiled back. All of my worries and fears for the past couple of days melted away with those four simple words from him. I leaned down and kissed him once again. I made sure it was gentle still because he was exhausted and his body wasn't in any condition to be doing anything physical. But my need to feel him connected to me was too strong. After a moment, I pulled back and kissed his forehead before I sat back.

"Move in with me. I know you are trying to get your own place and if that is what you want, then I will support you and respect your decision. But I don't want to waste any time that I'll get to spend with you. I want to go to sleep at night with you curled up in my arms. I

## JADED

want to wake up to you. I want everything in between, the good and the bad. Move in with me."

I was hoping he would say yes, but if he didn't, then I would respect that. I could understand him wanting to get his own place, to have a true home for the first time in his life. At the same time, though, I didn't want to live without him. I wanted to build a home with him.

"On one condition," he started weakly.

"Anything," I easily agreed. I didn't care what that condition was, I would be happy to agree to it.

"The curled up in your arms part, it starts now."

Now that was a condition I could live with and agree to all day. I instantly moved and crawled into the bed with him. Carefully, we got him turned so he was lying on his side against my chest. I wrapped my arms around him and placed a kiss to the top of his head as I spoke.

"Get some sleep, Baby. I'll be right here if you need me."

"I love you," he said, already sounding half-asleep.

"I love you, too."

If you had told me that I would eventually find a guy that I would be madly in love with, I would have denied it until I was blue in the face. I never thought I would ever be able to love another man. That I would ever be able to touch another man without feeling guilty and dirty.

Now here I was, about to start a new life with the man that I loved. It all felt

## JADED

like a dream, one I never wanted to wake up from. There was still work that needed to be done. Tyler would never truly be safe until Jasper was dead or in jail. But for tonight, I wasn't going to think about any of that. I was just going to enjoy the feeling of having the man that I love in my arms and think about the wonderful future that awaited us.

# EPILOGUE

Tyler

WE STUMBLED INTO our bedroom as Roland's lips devoured mine. We were finally going to get to do this. We were finally going to get to have sex.

The past month had been a huge challenge for the both of us. My lungs had healed up, but we were under strict orders by the doctor for me to not exert

## EVIE RILEY

myself for at least a month. I had to do breathing treatments just to get my lungs back to one hundred percent, or at least one hundred percent for me.

We hadn't been able to do much of any sexual activity outside of kissing. Tonight, though... Tonight was going to be different, because I was now officially cleared to resume normal activities.

We had both been counting down for this night. I knew Roland wanted to make it special, but I didn't care about that. All I wanted was his body and to finally feel him in me, against me. I didn't need anything special.

I just needed him.

Roland kicked the door closed. Mason and Koda were still living here until they found their own place in town. The task force was up and running and Mason

## JADED

was currently trying to find Jasper and the missing children. We rarely saw him, but he made a point of checking in on us and keeping us informed.

Roland pulled back, breaking the kiss, and I couldn't help but whine at the loss of contact. He smirked as he turned me around and I finally saw the room. He couldn't help the small chuckle at the sight of it. He had put candles all over the room, candles that were battery operated and not by flame. I'd had enough of fire for a lifetime and I knew he felt the same. There were also rose petals all over the bed and the floor. It was very sweet and only showed me how much he truly did love me.

"Look at you, being all romantic," I lightly teased as I pressed my ass back into his groin, causing him to moan.

# EVIE RILEY

"I told you, your first time should be special."

"It is special, because it's with you." I turned around and started to pull at his shirt as I continued. "But if you don't get naked, I'm going to play all by myself."

He spoke as he moved his hands over to the bottom hem of my shirt. "Now that is something I'd be happy to watch, but not tonight. Tonight, you are mine and I have every intention of keeping you very pleased all night long."

"That a promise?"

*God, I hope it was.*

"It's a guarantee," he said against my lips, but he didn't kiss me. Instead, he pulled back and my shirt quickly hit the floor. That was all we both needed before we swiftly rid the other of their pesky clothes and then, I was on my back on

## JADED

the bed with him on top of me.

I loved the feel of his weight against my body. It wasn't suffocating at all, but comforting and still, to this day, made me feel safe and wanted. I was his and I had no problem with that. Tonight, I was finally going to be his and only his, officially. He would be my first and I was hoping he would be my last.

Roland kissed his way down my neck as he ground his crotch against me, causing us both to moan. He continued to kiss his way down my chest and made sure to lick and suck on each of my nipples as he went further down until he reached my hard dick. He gave it a long lick along my shaft, causing me to instantly moan, before he took me down to my base in one go.

"Ro," I moaned as I moved my right

hand and tangled it in his hair.

This was only the second time he had given me oral sex and it was still just as amazing as the first time. I can't believe I had gone for so long without ever feeling this way. He continued to work his mouth along my dick, bringing me closer and closer to the edge.

"Oh fuck, I'm close." I couldn't help but thrust my hips up slightly to get even deeper inside of his mouth.

Roland didn't seem to mind, though, if the moan was anything to go by. His moan sent vibrations straight down my shaft and it pushed me over the edge. I came deep into his mouth and pulsed as he easily swallowed what I had for him. Once I had finished, he pulled his mouth off my dick with a pop. Kissing his way back up my body, he reached over and

## JADED

pulled out some lube from the bedside table.

"I need to stretch you so it doesn't hurt when I'm inside of you. It's going to feel a little weird, at first, but it will feel good. Trust me."

"I always trust you." The honesty in that sentence hit him and he flashed me a warm smile.

There was nothing that Roland could do that would take any trust away from him. He had more than earned my complete trust and faith in him, in and out of the bedroom. I wasn't sure what I expected, but it was not for him to grab me by my hips and flip us around.

He was lying down on his back with me on top of him, only I was facing the opposite direction of him. He seemed to have felt my confusion, because he

## EVIE RILEY

explained instantly.

"It'll be easier in this position for you. Plus, this way your mouth will be busy and it will distract you from the slight pain you might feel."

I wasn't sure what this was going to feel like, but I was happy for the distraction. I easily bent forward and sucked on his tip, tasting the precum that had been collecting. I felt one of his slicked up fingers circling my hole before he gently and slowly pushed it inside. It was a weird feeling, for sure, but I trusted that it would feel good soon enough.

I focused on making Roland feel good with my mouth as I took him down to his base. I did my best to focus on what I was doing and not the weird feeling of having Roland's finger moving in and out

## JADED

of me.

After a moment, he added a second finger and that one hurt slightly, but it wasn't too bad. I had only done a bit of research on gay sex and, apparently, I should have done more, but it seemed so straight forward at the time. Everything changed the second his fingers hit something inside of me and caused me to see stars. A deep moan escaped my lips.

"You like that, Baby? That's your sweet spot. Just think how good it is going to feel with my dick hitting it," Roland said as he made sure to hit that spot all over again.

I couldn't stop moaning at the pleasure that shot through me. My hips moved on their own accord as they pushed back, trying to take more of his

## EVIE RILEY

finger inside of me.

All too soon, he was adding a third finger and instead of pain, it only added to my pleasure. Once he felt that I was stretched enough, he removed his fingers from my hole and I moved my mouth off his dick.

Once again, his hands were on my hips and he flipped us around so he was sitting up with his back against the headboard, but I was straddling his lap facing him this time.

"Nice and slow, Baby. You control the pace, go as slow as you need."

He was letting me control how fast he was pushed inside of me and I loved him even more in this moment. He didn't need to be in control in the bedroom. He knew how much this moment mattered to me and he was allowing me go at my

## JADED

own pace.

It only made it more special.

Slowly, I lowered myself down onto him. The feel of his tip against my hole should have scared me, but it only turned me on. We were finally going to be connected. We were finally going to share something special and I knew it was going to be amazing and something we would both cherish for the rest of our lives.

Going slow and carefully, I lowered myself until his tip breached my hole and I took him inch by inch down to his base. Once he was fully inside of me, we both moaned and I kept myself still for a moment to adjust to his size. Roland began to slowly kiss me with a great deal of care and passion. We didn't need words, because the kisses said it all.

## EVIE RILEY

After a few minutes had passed and I was no longer feeling the sting, I slowly began to move up and down as Roland kissed his way along my neck. I wrapped my arms around his shoulders so I could better hold myself up as he placed his hands on my hips and angled them into a better position. I wasn't sure why, but the second I felt his tip hit my sweet spot, I couldn't stop the loud moan that erupted from me.

"I told you it would feel amazing," he said and flashed me a big smile.

*Amazing* didn't even come close to how that felt.

I continued to move slowly, but I did aim for that spot each time. With each second that passed, we were both moaning and riding on that edge. I wanted to feel him come inside of me.

## JADED

I needed to feel it.

Roland wrapped his arms around my hips and once again he flipped us, this time putting me on my back with him on top of me.

"You're loosened up enough, you ready to go to the moon?" he asked with a smirk.

"Hell yeah." I had no idea what he was going to do or how this could feel any better, but I was more than happy to find out.

He moved my legs so they were up on his shoulders. He slowly pulled out almost all of the way before he pushed back in, hitting my sweet spot in the process. That was the only slow thrust that he had, though, because after that his pace picked up rapidly. He repeatedly hit my sweet spot dead on, causing me to let out a scream as pleasure shot through me.

"That's it, Baby, let it out. Don't hold back."

"Oh fuck, don't stop. Harder." I moaned as I reached up and gripped the headboard behind me.

He was going to take me to the moon all right. My whole body was tingling from the pleasure he was giving me. He pushed as deep and as hard as he could each time and I had never felt so amazing before in my life. I never wanted this to end, but I could feel myself getting close and I could feel him getting close, too.

We had been waiting for this for a long time now and all that waiting was making us have short control. I knew Roland was close when he snaked a

## JADED

hand between us and started to touch my leaking dick.

"Shit, I'm close, Babe." I moaned.

"Come for me, Baby, I'm right behind you."

I couldn't hold off any longer and I gave a long and deep moan as I came, shooting it all over my stomach and chest. If I thought I was sensitive before, it was nothing compared to the feeling of pulsing while he continued to hit my sweet spot at a rapid pace.

I couldn't contain the soft screams as the pleasure shook through me. After another ten thrusts, Roland gave a final thrust and I felt him coming deep inside of me. He held still as he pulsed over and over again.

Both of us were breathing heavily and our bodies were covered in sweat and shaking. Roland leaned in and kissed me gently a few times as he lowered my legs. My whole body was shaking and I had no interest in moving at all. I didn't think I would be able to move, even if my life depended on it.

"Damn," Roland said softly as he broke the kiss and placed his forehead against mine.

"Damn, Damn," I agreed, flashing a big goofy smile.

There was nothing that could go wrong in this moment. It was perfect. Absolutely perfect. I had been dreaming about this moment since Roland first kissed me and my dreams didn't even come close to reality.

Reality was so much better.

Slowly, Roland pulled out of me and he managed to climb off the bed and

# JADED

head into the bathroom. By the time he came back, I hadn't managed to move.

"Did I break you?" he asked with a chuckle as he wiped away my stomach with a warm cloth.

"In all the right ways."

Once we were cleaned up, Roland turned the lights off and helped me to get under the covers before he joined me. I instantly rolled onto my side and curled up against his chest as he wrapped his arms around me.

"This was perfect. Thank you," I said as the drowsiness started to take over.

"You're perfect. I didn't hurt you right? You're okay?" he asked and I could hear the worry within his voice.

"You didn't hurt me, I'm good, Babe."

"You might be sore in the morning. We can always take a bath together."

## EVIE RILEY

"I'd like that."

I'd like to do anything that involved us both naked at this point. He was perfect.

The perfect man for me.

It's crazy when I think about how far we have come. I used to be terrified of him, I couldn't even look him in the eye, and now here we are. He was the man that I was madly in love with and wanted to spend the rest of my life with. The world operated in crazy ways, but I did believe that the world put people in your path that needed to be there and I was forever grateful that the world put Roland in my path.

I had no idea what the future was going to hold for us. Between our new relationship and Jasper still out there, any given moment could change

## JADED

anything.

What I did know, though, was I planned to embrace and cherish every moment that I could have with him and I knew he was going to do the same with me. I had always wanted a home. I just had no idea that my home was a person and not a building. Laying here in Roland's arms, I was finally home and it was more than I could have ever wished for.

Thank you for reading Jaded, book three in From the Edge.

If you enjoyed Jaded, please return to your retailer and leave a review. Even a few words can mean the world to an author. Plus it helps other readers like you find our work, too.
Share the love! ;)


Turn the page to read a preview from Rescue, the next book in the series.

# PREVIEW

Thad

*GOD DAMN IT.*

This was not a good start to the evening. I was running late, close to thirty minutes now, and I already knew my parents were going to be pissed at me over it. It was bad enough they were already going to be annoyed by my presence. I wasn't looking to make it

## EVIE RILEY

worse, but apparently the stars were not aligned with me tonight.

At the age of nineteen you would think I wouldn't be so worried about what my parents thought, but I wasn't worried about me. It was my kid brother, Danny, that held all of my concern. Growing up with very religious and strict parents was never easy, but it got increasingly dangerous when you were gay. Luckily for me, I didn't figure out my attraction to guys until recently. Danny, though, he hadn't been so lucky. He knew when he was twelve that he was gay. He kept it hidden, even from me, until he was fourteen.

I could still remember the night he told me as clear as day. I was seventeen and had been working a lot to save up for my own place. I wanted out of that

## JADED

house the moment I legally could. It was late and I heard him crying in his room. I wasn't about to walk away when I could tell he was in pain. That was never something we did with each other. Whenever we needed each other, the other was there.

No questions asked.

Growing up in a very strict home made us rely on each other for basic needs like comfort and love. Whenever one of us had a nightmare, we would go to the other. Whenever we were sick, the other one took care of them.

I was the one that walked him to and from school. I was the one that gave him baths. I was the one that would sneak him food when he didn't like whatever fancy crap our mother cooked. It was him and me against the world and I wouldn't change that.

Yes, it would have made my life easier if I hadn't had to practically raise my kid brother since I was eight, but he was my kid brother and I loved him. I wanted the best for him. It was just that simple.

So, when he was crying in his room, I instantly went in to see what had happened, what had upset him. He was a complete mess and hysterical from emotional pain.

It was that night that I discovered he was gay.

He was upset because our father had gone on a long rant about a gay guy he'd seen at church. He called the guy horrible names and those words cut deep in Danny.

I knew our parents would never accept him, they would do anything they

## JADED

could to force Danny to keep it hidden and to be straight. To me, though, I just wanted him happy. I didn't care who he loved as long as he got to experience it.

That night, I knew I wouldn't be able to leave him behind when I left. I started working even more to save up more so I could afford a two bedroom apartment. Once I turned eighteen, I moved out and Danny followed behind me six weeks later when he came out to our parents. They didn't handle it well and they kicked him out. That was eight months ago, and they had never reached out to him since.

I hadn't been so lucky.

They called every week to see if I had managed to convince my brother that he wasn't gay. They believed it was a phase or a hormone imbalance that was

## EVIE RILEY

causing him to feel the way that he did.

They had no idea.

To them, being attracted to the same sex was a mistake and God couldn't possibly make a mistake like that.

They would never accept him.

They would never accept me.

They didn't know I was gay.

I hadn't told anyone, not even Danny. It wasn't that I thought he wouldn't be okay with it, obviously he would be. It was more about me. I wasn't really ready to admit it out loud just yet. I was still adjusting to it all. Adjusting to my new reality and the new piece of myself.

Growing up, I had never looked at another guy like that before. Changing and showering in the locker room was nothing to me. I still didn't understand why all of a sudden I started checking

## JADED

out guys and watching gay porn.

I had started watching porn when I was seventeen, like most teenagers do, but it was always straight or girl on girl. The *typical guy* porn. The thing was, it never got me aroused. It was as if I watched a documentary on frogs or something. I chalked it up to not finding anything that interested me.

It wasn't until six weeks ago when I was feeling horny did I decide to try porn again. I just so happened to pick one that had a threesome with two guys. They were interacting with each other and, for the first time, I was able to orgasm while watching porn. The problem, though, I was busy watching the two guys and not the girl. That started to open up some questions, questions I was still dealing with. I could accept that I was gay. That wasn't too much of a big deal to me.

The problem was, I had no idea what to do about it. It was bad enough when I thought I was straight. I had been confused and self-conscious enough about sex when it was with a woman. I was nineteen and not only still a virgin, but I had never even been kissed.

My parents never allowed me to be alone with a girl. I had dated a couple in the past before I moved out, but I was always supervised. They believed that your first kiss should be at the altar. Now, I was a nineteen year old gold star virgin who was gay. It was a whole other world and I had no idea how to do any of it or how it would make me feel.

Was I a top or was I a bottom?

How would I know?

## JADED

What would I do if I didn't like giving oral sex or if I didn't want to be a bottom and the guy I was with was a top?

It was so much more complicated and I still wasn't ready to be active on it.

I let out a sigh as I parked in my parents' driveway. I wished I could have just turned around and gone home. I was exhausted from working so many hours this week.

I worked eighty hours every week, on average, just to be able to afford the apartment and have some money saved up for Danny's college education. He would have to get student loans as well, but at least he would have something that he could put toward it.

He wasn't sure what he wanted to do yet, but he was certain he didn't want to be a mechanic, like me. He wasn't

## EVIE RILEY

interested in working with his hands and he wasn't very good at it, either. He was more book smart than street smart, but that was okay. He deserved to go off to college and I wanted that for him. Even if that meant I worked more hours than I slept in the week.

My parents hated that I was a mechanic. They always had. Ever since I was little, I'd loved cars and being around them. I loved taking mechanical things apart and putting them back together. I used to do it all the time with the lawn mower. It drove them crazy, but I was always able to put it back together.

When I turned sixteen I used some of my money that I had saved up and bought this clunker of a car. My parents hated the thing and made me hide it in the garage so none of the neighbors

## JADED

would see it. I loved it, though, because I could spend all of my free time fixing it up and cleaning it. I had rebuilt the whole engine from parts I was able to pick up. To this day, I still drove it and you would never believe it was the same car.

When a position came up at one of two mechanic shops in town, I quickly grabbed it up and I'd never regretted it since. To my parents, though, I was a disgusting working class citizen. I was less of a man and person because I worked with my hands serving others. To them, I belittled myself because I choose to not work in an office like they did. It didn't matter to me, though. I loved it and I never wanted to do anything else. I hoped one day I could open my own shop and run my own

## EVIE RILEY

business.

Climbing out of my beloved car, I headed toward the door. I just needed to get this over and done with and then I could go home and relax with Danny. I knocked and waited for one of them to answer the door.

You would think with this being my parents' house that I could just walk right in, but I couldn't. I wasn't allowed to do that, because they found it disrespectful. As a guest, son or not, you waited until you were granted permission to enter the home. It was ridiculous, because I shouldn't be classified as a guest.

I was their son.

I should be able to walk right in.

With that being said, though, they were not allowed to just walk right into

## JADED

my apartment. But that wasn't because I wanted to be rude and make them feel like they had no control of the situation. It was because I worried they would try to grab Danny if they could come in whenever they wanted. I had gone out of my way to ensure that Danny felt safe at home and I was not about to jeopardize that.

The front door opened and my mother stood on the other side. She wore her perfectly ironed sundress with the matching kitten heels. Her hair and makeup were done as if she was going out to church instead of just having dinner at the house. She looked me up and down and I could tell she was disgusted by what she saw. I wore my work clothes so there was black grease on my pants. I had wanted to go home to change before coming over, but I had lost track of time working on a car and didn't have the chance to. At least, I had managed to get the grease off my hands.

"Hello, mother." Always *mother*, never mom. Just like it was always *father* and never dad. To them, anything less would be disrespectful.

"You couldn't have at least bothered to change?"

"I was working late and I didn't want to be any later than I already was. It's dry, it's not going to rub off on anything, mother."

That was another thing we were never allowed to do growing up, get anything dirty. Everything was always pristine. It had to be perfect in case anyone were to surprise us by coming by. It wasn't easy when you had two boys running around.

## JADED

We always had to be hyper vigilant with what we were doing outside. We couldn't play football after it rained, because if we dragged even a speck of mud into the house, we were stuck scrubbing the floors for hours until our mother was satisfied.

Always having to have the house immaculate growing up was why my apartment looked lived in. It wasn't dirty or messy, but when you walked in you knew people lived there. There was always a coat hanging over the back of a chair and there were dishes in the sink from breakfast. It was lived in and that was exactly how I liked it.

She let out a huff before she moved back and granted me permission to enter. I walked in and instantly removed my boots as she closed the door. There were no hugs or a kiss on the cheek. She would never allow it with me having dirt on my clothes. Even though it was dry and wouldn't transfer, she would never take that risk.

"Dinner is ready," she simply said as she turned on her kitten heels and headed off for the formal dining room.

I couldn't stifle the eye roll as I followed behind her. The formal dining room was always a sight to see. It was a long table, big enough for twenty people to sit at. It was often full for holiday parties that my parents would throw in extravagant fashion when we were growing up. It was always a big deal and the food was disgustingly fancy.

The type of food that a normal person would never eat.

I used to have to force it down, but

## JADED

Danny was never able to. It got to the point that my parents would have Danny up in his room for the parties and just make up some lie about why he couldn't be there. I used to sneak him up real food, normally a cheeseburger from some fast food joint.

One of the antichrists according to my parents.

Fast food and junk food was never supposed to be in the house. We were to have healthy food and only healthy food. Some kids would hide porno magazines under their bed.

We hid chocolate bars.

Of course, my father sat at the head of the table with my mother sitting next to him. I had no choice but to sit on the other side. The food was, thankfully, not that bad. It was chicken and vegetables,

## EVIE RILEY

at least.

"Good evening, father," I said as I sat down.

"You're late. A man of faith is never late."

"I'm sorry, father, Work ran late."

There was no point in telling him that a man of faith didn't kick his son out or disown him, either. Just like there was no point in telling him I hadn't stepped foot inside of a church since I left home on my eighteenth birthday last year.

He led saying grace before we were able to grab some of the food. I took a small portion because I knew my mother could barely cook. It might look good, but taste was a whole other beast.

"We need to talk about Daniel," my father started.

Apparently, we couldn't have a meal

## JADED

together as a family without some ulterior motive. I had suspected something was going on when my father had called and ordered me to come for dinner tonight. Normally, when they reached out to me it was over the phone and it was to tell me about some event that I was apparently obligated to attend. I never did, but they still felt the need to reach out to me and tell me. They felt like they could control me, still, and I was not about to let them feel that way. Whenever I could avoid it, I always did. Tonight, I knew something was going on because they had never invited me over for a family meal.

We didn't do family meals.

We did fake shows for the society they were connected to. If my parents wanted to sit down and share a meal with just me, they wanted something and I'd suspected it had to do with Danny.

"He's doing great. He's getting all A's in school," I said. I knew that wasn't what they wanted to talk about, but I was not about to just yield to what they wanted.

"Lord knows what he's doing for those A's," my mother said under her breath, and I was instantly pissed off.

Of course she would think that Danny was trading in deviant sexual favors in exchange for a better grade. It wasn't even the fact that she thought Danny would have to stoop that low, but that she thought he couldn't be smart enough to get straight A's without the help.

Not to mention, what kind of teachers

# JADED

did she think were at that school?

"We have tolerated this silly phase of his long enough. It's time to get serious. He needs to understand and see the light. He is not a queer. He is not a deviant living in sin. He needs to be cleansed of the demon inside of him and shown the light," my father lectured.

I was really getting sick of these beliefs of his. Homosexuality was only proof that demonic possession was real to him. It didn't matter how much scientific fact you provided him that sexual orientation was decided long before you were born. That it was within your genetic makeup and not some curse from God or the Devil trying to overtake your body.

"It's genetic, father. He can't control being gay anymore than you can control being straight."

"Deviant behaviors can be controlled and corrected. I have reached out to a man that runs a facility that is equipped to handle this very situation. He runs a highly successful conversion camp and he has a place for Daniel."

A cold dread flooded my body.

He wanted to have my kid brother sent to a conversion camp?

*Hell no.*

I had heard of those places. It wasn't like a bible study group. They used any means necessary to try and rewire a person's brain to believe they were straight. They were taught how to suppress a major part of who they were just so they could fit in with what society dictated for a man to be. Danny couldn't go to a place like that. I wasn't going to

# JADED

let that happen.

"You can't send him to a place like that. Father, do you know what things they do to the kids there?"

He couldn't actually be educated properly on this. There was no way he would be willing to risk sending his own son there. They used any type of methods to "save" the boys there. Including sleep deprivation, starvation, abuse, borderline torture, and more. There was a reason the camps had been getting shut down whenever one was discovered.

"I am well aware of what goes on in the facility. I've already toured it. Daniel will learn how to be a real man and to finally be rid of this ridiculous phase. He will return to be a man of God and live how our Father wanted him to. It is on you to ensure he is here Saturday morning and ready to go. He doesn't need a bag, they will provide the proper clothing."

He actually thought I would not only agree to this, but to gift wrap my baby brother for them. That I could somehow convince him it was a good idea. He was more insane than I thought. There was no way I was going to allow this to happen. I would to do whatever I had to to ensure Danny was safe.

I'd stupidly thought they would just leave us alone. Allow Danny to stay with me until he was eighteen and then he would be an adult so it wouldn't matter. Now, though, I could see our father was not about to let that happen. He was not going to risk someone finding out that he had a gay son.

## JADED

It looked like I was going to have to do something I had hoped to avoid, but now it seemed like the only way to save Danny from that level of pain. I would have to file for custody of him and fight my parents in court for him.

This dinner looked like it would be the last supper for our family. Because coming morning, it was going to be a bloody fight. One I was hoping Danny and me would survive.

Snag your copy of Rescue at your favorite online retailer.

If you enjoyed Jaded, the third book in the From The Edge series, please return to your retailer and leave a review. Even a few words can mean the world to an author. Plus it helps other readers like you find our work too.

Share the love! ;)

# OTHER BOOKS BY EVIE

**Federal Protection Agency**
Mason
Rafe
Ryzen
Cooper
Noah
Damien
Sebastian
Gabe
Logan

**Ruthless Empire**
Courting Danger
Chasing Danger
Kissing Danger

**Smokejumpers**
Hawke
Cyrus
Jase
Gage
Jackson
Xavier

## Jasper Springs
Cade
Dawson
Drew
Grayson
Riley
Mitch

## From The Edge
Shattered
Runaway
Jaded
Rescue
Hidden
Tormented

## Gray Vale Pack
His Fated Mate
His Wounded Warrior
His Healing Heart

# ABOUT THE AUTHOR

Evie Riley is a prolific, neurodivergent author known for her captivating MM romance novels. She has gained a significant following and topped the LGBT+ action and adventure bestseller charts with her series.

Evie's writing style often explores dark and gritty themes where her men must overcome difficult obstacles in their search for love, but she has also ventured into sweeter small-town romances, incorporating tropes like enemies-to-lovers, friends-to-lovers, age-gap, and forced proximity. She is known for crafting engaging romantic suspense novels and has a knack for creating interconnected series worlds that keep readers invested.

# EVIE RILEY

Interestingly, Ms. Riley has hinted at exploring new genres, such as Alien Omegaverse Romance, in the future.

Outside of writing, she enjoys spending time at the beach and has a quirky personality, described by her partner as ranging from cute to deadly, depending on her blood-chocolate levels.

Evie spends her nights writing bad boys in love, and her days wrangling the sweet boys she loves.

www.ingramcontent.com/pod-product-compliance
Lightning Source LLC
Chambersburg PA
CBHW072145070526
44585CB00015B/999